TREASURED TRADITION

robin brown

TREASURED TRADITION

Treasured Tradition: Delaware State Fair Centennial — 100 Years of Family Fun

By robin brown, Delaware Public Archives Writer-in-Residence

Design by robin brown & Doug Williams

Photo editing by Danny Aguilar

Published by The Delaware State Fair Inc., Copyright 2019
In cooperation with the Delaware Public Archives

ISBN: 978-1-7335840-1-2

CONTENTS

100 YEARS OF FAMILY FUN

WELCOME TO THE Delaware State Fair Centennial!
Thank you for being part of this all-American tradition of family fun in the First State.

Our modern fair, this year marking its 100th anniversary, is one of the oldest, most popular and most successful events of its type in the country.

And, with weather-permitting annual attendance of about 300,000 – close to a third of the state population – it's Delaware's biggest annual attraction.

"I love the state fair," Governor John Carney said. "It's amazing, always a lot of fun for families, and it shows off the best of our state – our people, our history and our future. ...And there's always something new to see every year," he added. "I wouldn't miss it."

To walk around its expansive fairgrounds in Harrington in the state's heartland Kent County – where Governor's Day gives everyone a chance to meet our highest elected official – it's hard to imagine that the modern fair we all know began a full century ago.

Its competitions draw tens of thousands of entries from cattle to crochet. Top music performers and special events

Left: Delaware State Fair General Manager William J. DiMondi
Right: Delaware State Fair President R. Ronald Draper

such as the demolition derby and monster trucks regularly get sell-out crowds. The popular midway screams with the latest thrill rides and prize games for all ages. Exhibitors and agencies – known for their freebies – show off their latest services and equipment. The Marketplace offers everything from bamboo sheets and basement waterproofing to bird feeders and baby dresses. Many Delaware businesses lend support through sponsorships that provide free entertainment and services from a petting zoo to diaper-changing station.

Meanwhile, an ever-evolving lineup of attractions keeps fairgoers finding new fun and food such as alligator bites on a stick, octo-tacos stuffed with real octopus, the trademark Delaware Dog loaded with authentic Kirby and Holloway scrapple and deep-fried candy bars that have become a popular standard.

The fair's fare has been so wild, in fact, that it has starred on the national "Carnival Eats" television show. The fair also wins recognition in various lists of the country's top state fairs, even some that mix in county and regional events.

Ron Draper, president of the Delaware State Fair Board of Directors, says the fair's success is multi-faceted including both consistency and change.

In addition to keeping true to its agricultural roots and being blessed with incomparably dedicated volunteers and staff, he said the fair has been willing to try

new things while maintaining its values and successful traditions. That means fairgoers can come find their old favorites, but enjoy something new every year.

Also, Draper said, fair activities have adapted to an increasingly evening-oriented public.

Both day and night, many on the Harrington fairgrounds who are asked to name their favorite part of the Delaware State Fair reply with the same simple answer:

"Everything."

Grown from its initial four days to its current 10-day run, the modern Delaware State Fair maintains deep agricultural roots – but has been developed to maintain public interest and stability.

Avoiding pitfalls of financial problems and flagging public interest that ultimately doomed nearly a dozen other early fairs statewide – closing after runs of three to 23 years – the nonprofit Delaware State Fair has reached its 100th anniversary with fiscal stability and strong attendance, prompting big thanks from its organizers to everyone who ever "spent a day at the fair."

Over the decades, the fair would not have been possible, lasting or secure for the future without vital support from a myriad of Delawareans who have and continue to contribute directly to its annual presentation, from members of the Delaware General Assembly and other elected officials to exhibitors, vendors and advertisers, organizers say.

For a century, the largest ranks of fair supporters have been filled with its uncounted fair presidents, vice presidents and other officers, directors, managers, committee members and department superintendents, staff members and thousands upon thousands of other volunteers who have worked tirelessly year-round behind the scenes and during the fair – year after year after year – to keep it safe, fresh and fun for the whole extended Delaware State Fair family.

Harrington Mayor Anthony R. Moyer considers the secret of the fair's longevity and success to be its "community feel."

"The state fair is Delaware and that's why people love it so much and keep coming back," said Delaware Public Archives Director Stephen M. Marz. "It's about our history, our life, our memories," he said, adding that the fair reminds him of childhood days riding a goat named Billy.

"The fair shares the story of who we were, who we are and a remarkable century of our life in Delaware," Marz said.

And the fair demonstrates how much the community cares, said Patricia Beebe, president and chief executive officer of the Food Bank of Delaware that benefits from the fair's annual Food Lion Hunger Relief Day donation drive.

"The Delaware State Fair is such an integral part of the landscape of Delaware and such a rich part of Delaware history," Beebe said. "We are proud to be a part of a community that is so generous by giving back to their neighbors in need."

She and others involved in the fair view the fair's centennial as cause for celebration. "We wish the Delaware State Fair congratulations on celebrating their first 100 years and we look forward to being a part of writing the history of the next 100 years," Beebe said.

To commemorate the century mark, the Delaware State Fair organization is proud to publish and share this celebratory book in honor of all fair supporters who have passed away and with deepest gratitude to all who are or have been part of its enduring success.

The Delaware State Fair Centennial – with many special activities, souvenirs and a special logo banner boasting "A Century of Family Fun" – also is being honored with an engaging, interactive exhibit at the Delaware Public Archives in Dover, exploring and sharing the fair's history and heritage.

Thanks to the support of state lawmakers, the fair's 100th anniversary also is being recognized with the historic issuance of a limited edition centennial license plate that is perhaps the ultimate Delaware State Fair collectible.

And to think it all began with a few friends gathered around a pot belly stove.

Main St., Harrington, Del.

Commerce St., Harrington, Del.

THE FAIR IS BORN

Harrington's railroad station was the kind of place where folks would go for more than travel.

They would go to see what was arriving in or going out on the rail cars. They might stop by to see who had produce to sell or trade. Or they might go to hear about community goings-on, catch up on gossip or swap some news from out-of-town.

Or they might sit around the pot-belly stove and pass the time of day with friends.

A few townsfolk were doing just that one day in 1919 – or so the story goes – when they started talking and dreaming big.

They were dreaming of starting a fair.

After the wild success of the 1876 Centennial Exposition in Philadelphia,

fairs had become big throughout the country, growing from their origins as medieval European markets to full-blown community entertainment.

At the time, there was no shortage of fairs in the region. There was a well-established one operating in New Castle County and four others in nearby Maryland and Pennsylvania.

But the handful of men meeting in Harrington thought southern Delaware deserved one of its own.

As they chatted about the idea in ever-increasing detail in both planned and impromptu meetings at the station, they didn't record details of their talks – or even exactly who was there.

Later accounts said they tried to keep their meetings secret.

But small towns being small towns, word spread. And the idea of the fair became all the talk.

Soon, there were too many people interested in the idea of a fair – from business folk to farmers – for them to meet in the train station, so their gatherings shifted to the fire hall.

KENT & SUSSEX COUNTY FAIR ASSOCIATION, INC.
Harrington, Del.

Five
Big
Days

Five
Big
Nights

"FAIR COMRADES"

July 24, 25, 26, 27, 28, 1923

In January 1920, the group incorporated as the Kent & Sussex County Fair Association.

Charles D. Murphy – identified in later records as the fair founder, the main force behind its creation or one of its founding fathers – was chosen as the group's founding president, one of three Harrington residents leading the charge.

At his side were Vice President Ora Sapp, Secretary Ernest Raughley and Treasurer William Smith.

Harrington residents who joined them as founding fair directors were H.E. Quillen, S.O. Bailey, George H. Brown, John H. Bullock, W.S. Cahall, Frank Graham, John H. Holloway, W.E. Jacobs, Lorenzo T. Jones, Warren T. Moore, Alda B. Powell, B.I. Shaw, John W. Sheldrake, Joshua Smith, W.A. Smith, W.S. Smith, Earl Sylvester and Charles S. Warren.

Bridgeville was the next most-represented area with directors Norman Collison, Warren Newton and William J. Swain. Dr. J.B. Derrickson and John Sipple joined the board from Frederica. Filling out the ranks were J.M. Harrington of Felton, Charles Henrietta of Clayton, Harry McDaniel of Dover, F.M. Sopher of Wyoming, Henry Stafford of Burrsville, John Todd of Greenwood and Harry Windsor of Milford.

The founding board – destined to grow in time to 80 members – raised money by selling 1,200 shares of capital stock at $25 apiece, with stock subscriptions explaining that the purpose was "to have or manage a Fair or Exposition for the purpose of promoting and encouraging Agriculture and of giving pleasures and diversions to the inhabitants of rural communities within the State of Delaware."

The fair stock wouldn't pay dividends then – or ever. That was part of the deal.

When the board had raised enough through sale of the no-dividend shares, later to become family treasures mainly handed down through generations, they made their first big investment.

They spent $6,000 to buy 30 acres of clear, flat farmland from William S. and Nellie Smith just south of town. The purchase of that land – even century later, still at the heart of the fairgrounds – was finalized on February 17, 1920.

The fair was set for a four-day run – that July 27 through 30 – less than six months away, with no time to waste. To this day, the fair consistently has been held the last week in July.

Volunteers organized quickly, with J.M. Harrington organizing races, W.S. Smith supervising the grounds, John Holloway managing the grandstands and Lane Adams in charge of police and concessions. Other superintendents were charged with the various departments. W.D. Scott had poultry, C.S. Warren had cattle. Alfred Raughley

supervised horses while W.A. Smith had sheep and swine. Fruit and Dairy were handled by F.M. Sopher and Joshua Smith, machinery.

In the since-abandoned custom of the day, female superintendents were identified only by their husbands' names – Mrs. J.W. Sheldrake for the exhibit hall, Mrs. W.S. Smith and Mrs. Will Powell for the "Ladies Department," the lone exceptions being needlework superintendents Alice Wix and Elizabeth McCabe.

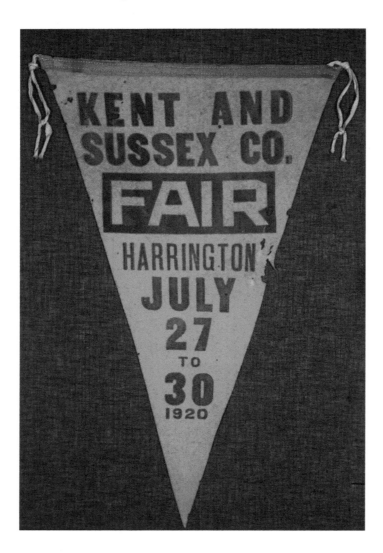

Krause Greater Shows was hired for the midway, boasting 12 big shows, 30 concessions, three mechanical rides and three kinds of free entertainment. Bennie Krause, the carnival manager, promised he would be present for all four days of the fair – promising that any "rough" or "immoral stuff" would be prohibited and he would allow nothing but "high-class" amusements.

Admission was set at 50 cents with half-price for kids. But there was a 3-cent "war tax" required on public entertainment that the fair couldn't waive. So that was added to every ticket. And unlike today, when the fair maintains a policy of free parking, a 25-cent parking fee was charged for "rigs, automobiles and motorcycles" – plus another 3 cents for the obligatory war tax on parking.

The quickly printed premium book listed prizes and competitions, initially open to only Kent and Sussex county residents.

Although winning entries would bring their owners ribbons and cash prizes, the buck stopped there.

The fair's superintendents and officers, like other directors including those chosen to serve on the executive committee, would not receive any pay. Neither would their dozens of friends, family members and neighbors who pitched in at the fairgrounds.

Horse racing was a main attraction, with about 150 horses, and a later news account observing that "horsemen and jockeys alike have nothing but a good word."

On two of the four nights, big motorcycle races wowed the crowds – and the winners who took home big prizes. First-place finishers won $50, second-place earned $25 and third-place got $15. But every rider earned a participants' fee of $5 – the modern equivalent of slightly more than $65.

The only reported problem was that the heat prompted a few women to faint, but they quickly were treated by the Red Cross Motor Corps.

At the close of the first fair, its total attendance was estimated at about 15,000 from throughout Delaware, Maryland and Virginia.

The fair association "expressed its full appreciation of the patronage, given the fair in its infancy and first attempt."

Little could the founding directors have imagined that the fair's total attendance would hit hundreds of thousands, growing from a number equaling less than 7 percent of Delaware's population to nearly a third of the resident total. Or could they have dreamed that the grounds gradually would grow to more than 300 acres, that fair entries would

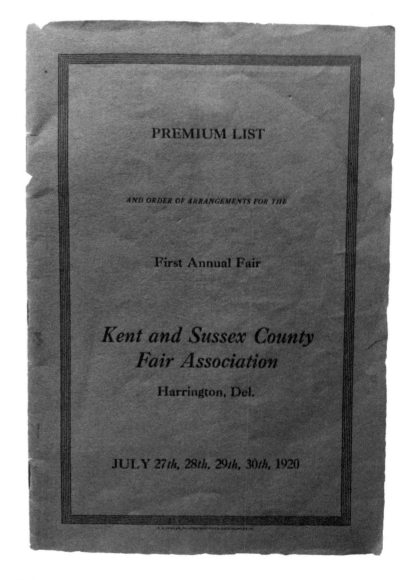

PREMIUM LIST

AND ORDER OF ARRANGEMENTS FOR THE

First Annual Fair

Kent and Sussex County Fair Association

Harrington, Del.

JULY 27th, 28th, 29th, 30th, 1920

skyrocket from a few hundred to tens of thousands, that legalized gambling someday would finance repairs and construction or that running the fair would take fulltime employees, require year-round planning and become a multi-million-dollar operation?

On closing day of the first fair, Milford Chronicle headlines proclaimed the event a success that would become permanent – "Evidenced by the Commendable Attractions and Large Attendance."

Harrington's Big Annual Event

The Great

KENT AND SUSSEX FAIR

Harrington, Del.

FIVE BIG DAYS | **July 26 to July 30** | **FIVE BIG NIGHTS**

The Most Elaborate Program Ever

HERE'S THE BIG PROGRAM

TUESDAY—CHILDREN'S DAY

There will be no admission charged for children under 16 years of age on this day. Grandstand free to everybody. Children admitted to grounds free at night. Entertainment day and night. 2:13 Pace, 2:30 Trot, 2:22 Pace, Mule Races, Vaudeville Acts.

WEDNESDAY

The fastest racing of the week. $1,000.00 Free-For-All, 2:30 Pace, 2:22 Trot. High Class Acts in front of the Grandstand day and night.

BRUCE'S GREATER SHOWS

Consisting of

Merry-Go-Round, Whip, Ferris Wheel, Merry-Mix-Up Baby Seaplane, Miniature Railroad.

Kelly's Wonderland Sideshow, Bruces Greater Minstrels, Capt. Bertram Thomas Museum, Smith's Freakland, Midget Village, Wallace Reptile Exhibit, Erby Congress Athletes, Monkey Speedway, Mercer's Motordrome, Superbs, Palace of Illusions.

Will be one of our Big Attractions every afternoon and evening.

THURSDAY—THE BIG DAY

For everybody. SURPRISES will come fast. Big Live Stock Parade. 2:20 Trot, 2:17 Pace, 2:12 Trot, 2:25 Pace.

FRIDAY

The Lucky Day, when friends, farmers, and politicans meet. The last day of horse racing. 2:20 Pace, 2:16 Trot, 2:25 Trot and Running Races.

SATURDAY

Professional — Sanctioned

Auto Races

World's Greatest Drivers
World's Fastest Cars

A REAR COMPETITIVE CONVENTION of Speed

6——BIG EVENTS——6

Sanctioned by the
Contest Board of the American Automobile Association

RALPH A. HANKINSON, Director of Contests

THE LAST DAY—THE BIG DAY

MULE RUNNING RACES Tuesday, All colored drivers. HORSE RUNNING RACES, Friday, all white drivers. Conditions of Races – Two half mile heats, purse $100.00. All Post Entries. No entrance fee. Four moneys divided, $50, $25, $15, $10.

Get your mules and horses ready and mail entries to Ernest Raughley, Secretary, Harrington, Delaware

CALIFORNIA FRANK'S WILD WEST RODEO

Performs Daily---Many other attractions added since last year.

Just days after the first fair, the founders' initial accounting to the public said expenditures had topped $30,000, but that they had a total of about $15,000 in receipts.

Finally, when all the adding and subtracting was finished, the fair reported a first year profit.

That profit was a whopping $43.90 and a lasting reminder for directors to remember to spend wisely and, even in hard economic times, keep the fair within its means to protect its future.

As its supporters planned the second annual event, and preparations made their first step toward a year-round nature, the fair adopted a slogan that would stand for many years – "Bigger and Better Than Ever."

For its second year, the fair expanded to five days in duration. That second year saw construction and dedication of its new State Exhibition Hall built by the State of Delaware, addition of automobile racing, the fair's first fireworks and the introduction of the Boys and Girls Club Department, precursor of today's 4-H Department.

And while decades would pass before adoption of its modern name, advertising for the second annual Kent and Sussex County Fair unabashedly broadened its horizons, declaring the event "OPEN TO THE WORLD!"

The fair proved popular, but also part of a growing trend. By the time 1923 rolls around, the region had become home to a total of eight such events – almost all in the summertime.

FAIR VIEW PARK, DOVER, DEL.

In addition to Harrington, fair sites included Wilmington/Elsmere, where one ran August 27 through 31; Cambridge, Maryland, running July 31 through August 3; Tasley, Virginia, with activities August 7 through 10; Pocomoke, Maryland, with an August 14-17 event; Salisbury, Maryland, with its fair August 21-24, and West Chester, Pennsylvania, with the latest of the fairs, held October 2-6.

These and other fairs would come and go at sites scattered throughout the region.

THE GREATER DELAWARE STATE FAIR
Wawaset Park, Wilmington, Delaware   September 7, 8, 9, 10, 11, 1914

Greetings from Kent & Sussex Fair

P. B. & W. Railroad Depot, Harrington, Del.

But this one that sprouted in 1920 from seeds of chit-chat at a small town railroad station and grew into our Delaware State Fair would be the only one to endure strong enough and long enough to celebrate its 100th anniversary.

PUTTING HARRINGTON ON THE MAP

Harrington is best known as the home of the Delaware State Fair. Before that, however, it was the railroad that put Harrington on the map – literally – and helped bring the fair to town.

The community first was called Clark's Corner after Benjamin Clark, who built a tavern and home in 1780 at Milford and Frederica roads. His inn grew into a trading post, stagecoach stop and spot where the region's residents shared the latest news.

Still, Dover-born Samuel Maxwell Harrington would have an even greater influence.

Harrington served 35 years as a Delaware justice, including terms as chief justice, and was a main force behind the state staying in the Union during the Civil War.

His decisions included those covering the status of freed slaves and the nation's first independent African-American churches in Wilmington.

But it was his railroad advocacy that changed the town.

Harrington championed the effort to charter and finance the Delaware Railroad. He also oversaw its construction, linking the state's northern and southern regions.

A railroad junction added at Clark's Corner in 1856 forever changed the town. Business boomed as did the population at the later-incorporated spot that earned a nickname as "The Hub of Delaware."

In Harrington's honor, the town adopted his name in 1862.

More than half a century later, the rail station bearing Harrington's name also would be where chatting residents decided to start the modern state fair and where its attractions first arrived.

"I remember, as a kid, hearing the train and looking out my bedroom window when the fair came to town," said Doug Poore of the Harrington Historical Society. Watching the rail cars unload their exotic cargo "was very exciting," he said.

His mother, Viva Poore, remembers the fair as early as 1949, when she moved to Harrington.

"I don't think I've missed a year," she said with a big smile and smidge of pride.

A fair volunteer for more than 50 years, she recalls working an early admission gate that she operated by a foot pedal to let in one patron at a time.

In the 1950s, she said, "the whole town would shut down and all the businesses closed ... because everybody was at the fair."

Her church, St. Stephen's Episcopal, was one of many community groups to benefit. "That's how we paid for our new church building was selling food at the fair," she said.

The fair's impact has been immense on Harrington, where the population was 1,617 in

Exhibit Buildings - Delaware State Fair - 1935

the event's opening year and last estimated by the U.S. Census as 3,562.

The last financial impact study in 1996 estimated that the fair brings about $4 million a year into the Harrington area – equal to nearly $6.4 million today.

The fair each year hires about 200 residents, Harrington Mayor Anthony R. Moyer confirmed, and vendors provide even more jobs.

Beyond fair jobs, Moyer added, the fair is "a time of pride" for area youngsters who work all year with sheep, cows, other animals and projects to exhibit.

The fairgrounds also boosts Harrington with its growing calendar of year-round activities – including horse shows, live harness racing, car shows and flea markets – along with a popular public ice-skating rink that is open 10 months of the year.

The town that covers just 2.75 square miles also has bragging rights as home to the nation's oldest continuously operating harness racing track, thanks to the fair.

Enthusiasts started harness racing at the fairgrounds track in 1946, then formed their own association and built the current track. The site was bolstered by a change in state gambling laws that allowed the opening of a video lottery slot machine casino there in 1996.

Harrington Raceway & Casino attracts about 150,000 visitors and does about $10 million in business monthly, spurring motel and restaurant development.

The $6 million casino by law supports the state's general fund and horse-racing improvements, also providing about 800 jobs. With most of those positions filled locally, Moyer said, "the raceway is a key employer for Harrington."

Although now run separately, the raceway-casino wouldn't be there if not for the state fair.

It's one of a growing number of businesses – also including The Centre Ice Rink, where bumper cars on-ice are all the rage – that dot the fairgrounds, grown over the years to nearly 300 acres.

And with the town used to handling the traffic and guests of the state fair's 10-day run, even with increasingly popular evening events and concerts by big name performers, Moyer said, "There's no negative impact whatsoever."

Sometimes, however, folks who are in too much of a hurry to get to the fair or go home may end up with a little negative-impact souvenir they would rather not have.

That's because the police departments in Camden, Felton, Harrington and Greenwood all take strict enforcement of their local speed limits seriously. So fair organizers encourage guests to take their time – both coming and going – to avoid overly hasty travel to prevent speeding tickets and three points on their driving records.

Besides, obeying local speed limits gives drivers the chance to look around a bit and better appreciate these local municipalities.

And as the fair celebrates its centennial, its host town will celebrate its incorporation 150 years ago.

"We'll be cooperating with the fair to celebrate both our anniversaries," the mayor said, adding that, in addition to its economic benefits, the fair always creates its own unique excitement and vitality.

"We love to have it here," he added. "Harrington wouldn't be on the map if it wasn't for the state fair."

List of Stock Holders Kent & Sussex Co Fair
Harrington, Delaware, Jan 1928

Name	Shares		Name	Shares	
W H Cahall	4	P	George Cannon	1	a
James Cahall	4	a	Joshua Smith	4	a
A C Creadick	12	a	Oscar Hill	1	a
Asa Bennett	6	a	Henry Hill	20	a
G H Brown	2	a	W S Smith	20	a
B B Bowden	1	a	John Masten	1	a
Charlie Neeman	2	P	B A Shaw	13	a
J D Clark	2	a	Mrs J C Capp	10	a
C D Murphy	26	a	L J Jones	4	a
W J Poskey	8	P	L B Harrington	10	a
John J Harrington	2	a	W E Jacobs	10	a
Chas H Jacobs	1	a	Ira Killen	2	a
F L Masten	4	a	Hollis Dodd	2	a
C E Hurley	2	a	Wm Hughes	2	a
Wm Masten	4	a	Gillis Brittingham	1	a
Wilbur B Payton	1	a	Walter Hughes	1	a
A W Warren	10	a	J E Halliday	1	a
J Roy Cannon	2	P	J M Harrington	8	a
Horace E Quillen	22	P	Henry Austin	1	a
Arthur Collison	1	a	Samuel Md. Marshall	1	a
Robert Ross	1	a	Windsor	4	a
Smith & Roughley	5	a	W A Webb	7	a
Mrs Elizabeth H Poole	4	a	J F Graham	2	a
Mrs Annie Cannon	1	a	W T Moore	7	a

Original stockholders

Ætna Insurance Company letterhead, Hartford, Connecticut

MORE THAN A CENTURY OF SERVICE — AETNA — HARTFORD, CONN. — INCORPORATED 1819 — CHARTER PERPETUAL

RALPH B. IVES, PRESIDENT

EDGAR J. SLOAN, VICE-PRESIDENT
GUY E. BEARDSLEY, VICE-PRESIDENT AND SECRETARY
W. ROSS McCAIN, VICE-PRESIDENT AND SECRETARY
J. R. STEWART, SECRETARY
GEORGE L. BURNHAM, TREASURER
W. C. ROACH, ASSISTANT SECRETARY

S. W. CORNWELL, ASSISTANT SECRETARY
P. W. D. JONES, ASSISTANT SECRETARY
J. M. WALLER, ASSISTANT SECRETARY
FRANK G. BUSH, ASSISTANT SECRETARY
WELLINGTON H. WART, ASSISTANT SECRETARY
M. W. MORRON, MARINE SECRETARY

H. E. (SQUIRE) QUILLEN, AGENT

Harrington, Delaware,

Name		Name	
D B Tharp	10	Mollie E Warren	2
Everett J Messick	4	Ernest B Raughley	1
P. Reese Layton	1	Warren C Newton	2
Harry Cannon	4	Thomas Minner	12
A W Dowrry	4	L. D. Harrington	4
W W Sharp	10	Samuel Creadick	2
Wm J Swain	4	J P Masten	10
Norman Collison	4	Henry Stafford	10
E J Elliott	4	John H Halloway	1
Mrs Bertha Rosh	4	Harry B Johnson	4
Saunders M Truitt	1	Mrs Cora Collison	1
J R Elliott	4	John F Ferris	1
Lawrence Deeman	1	Marion L Beck	1
Mrs Alfred Raughley	4	I S Short Lumber Co	20
John B Derrickson	2	J A Gray	1
John Dipple	2	Robert Jarrell Jr	4
D J Minner	2	J O Bailey	1
J H Massey	12	W B Fleming	6
W S Booth	4	George E Morris	1
Clarence Voshell	5	Harry Harrington	4
J W Kemp	4	William Creadick	1
Edgar N Dill	4	Herman Johnson	1
Samuel Tharp	2	J S Townsend Jr	2

Original stockholders

RALPH B. IVES, PRESIDENT

EDGAR J. SLOAN, VICE-PRESIDENT
GUY E. BEARDSLEY, VICE-PRESIDENT AND SECRETARY
W. ROSS MCCAIN, VICE-PRESIDENT AND SECRETARY
J. R. STEWART, SECRETARY
GEORGE L. BURNHAM, TREASURER
W. C. ROACH, ASSISTANT SECRETARY

S. W. CORNWELL, ASSISTANT SECRETARY
P. W. D. JONES, ASSISTANT SECRETARY
J. M. WALLER, ASSISTANT SECRETARY
FRANK G. BUSH, ASSISTANT SECRETARY
WELLINGTON H. WART, ASSISTANT SECRETARY
M. W. MORRON, MARINE SECRETARY

Ætna Insurance Company
HARTFORD, CONNECTICUT

H. E. (SQUIRE) QUILLEN, AGENT

Harrington, Delaware,

Name	Shares	
Chas S. Richards	2	A
Frank A. Elliott	4	B
Geo. Dewey Sapp	2	B
John W. Abdereke	1	B
Andrew J. Lynch	1	A
Mrs. Elva Krull	1	B
John M. Willey	2	A
George H. Hearn	4	A
Dr. H. E. Thomison	1	A
L. D. Caulk	4	B
J. Harold Schabinger	2	B
Dr. W. T. Chipman	4	B
C. F. Wilson	10	B
Josiah A. Beck	2	A
J. Gordon Smith	4	A
Frank Vangesel	2	B
L. E. Hardley	4	B
Edith M. Bryan	2	B
	504	
(112)		

Original stockholders

RECEIPTS AND EXPENDITURES OF KENT & SUSSEX COUNTY FAIR, 1927

CASH RECEIVED

Cash balance from 1926	144.68	
Carnival Concessions	3,700.00	
All other concessions	1,807.39	
Dupont Fund a/c Boys & Girls Club Bldg.	520.20	
Appropriation from State for Premiums	5,157.79	
Net Receipts from Farm	71.05	
From Sale of Manure	37.50	
Sundries	5.86	
Gate and Grand Stand	23,673.40	
Entrance Fees - Poultry 117.50		
Horses 2,896.50	3,014.00	
Net Receipts from Sweepstake Race	352.42	
Net Receipts from 4th of July Races	895.39	
Notes Payable	1,000.00	$40,469.68

EXPENDITURES

Notes paid off from 1926	$ 5,250.00	
Interest	352.33	
Electric Light, New Wiring & Poles	656.86	
Office Rent	50.00	
Expense 1927 Banquet	226.10	
Sec'y. & Treas. Salary	700.00	
Office Help	132.75	
Advertising	1,109.88	
Judges and their expenses	274.85	
Taxes	210.00	
Insurance	553.56	
Boys and Girls Club Bldg.	5,675.00	
Premiums	5,166.79	
Upkeep Grounds	1,702.68	
Upkeep Track	300.80	
Straw Account	591.88	
Secretary's expenses	69.48	
General Expense	211.01	
Help: Ticket Sellers, Police, etc., during Fair	1,233.59	
Permanent Improvement	259.49	
Stationery, Tickets, etc.	338.14	
Attractions -		
Vaudeville & Music 3,850.00		
Fireworks 924.14		
Auto Races 1,500.00		
Mule & Pony Races 250.00	6,524.14	
Stakes (Inc. entrance money)	8,671.25	$40,253.58
Balance..$216.10		

Comparative Receipts	Grand Stand and Gate	Appropriations, Privileges, etc.
1920	$10,206.28	$11,083.43
1921	13,151.56	8,775.28
1922	14,526.07	9,111.23
1923	14,874.88	9,192.50
1924	19,343.60	9,863.99
1925	22,795.67	11,722.60
1926	19,883.50	11,968.71
1927	23,673.40	15,651.60

Profit & Loss statement from 1927

FACES AT THE FAIR

NED MAULL OF Lewes has been coming to the fair for 71 years. His mother was from Harrington and his great-grandfather, who had a farm west of Harrington, always raced horses.

"We always came to the fair because it was part of life in our area at the time," he said.

And ever since he can remember, the same part of the fair has always been his favorite.

"The people," he said. "I enjoy talking to the people."

Maull has many friends who help organize and run the fair, although he is not a director himself.

He also enjoys running into other friends, neighbors and acquaintances at the fair and likes the kind of friendly chat among strangers that is typical while perusing entries and exhibits or enjoying a little bite to eat. And it's an idea that seems to run in his family.

His 6-year-old granddaughter, Elizabeth Mills of Milton, first said Twiggs the giraffe was her favorite part of the fair.

But she thought about it for a moment and changed her mind to agree with Maull.

"No, I think he's right," she said. "I like the people best, too."

LOVING THE FAIR

Donna Ratledge and her daughter Mary, who live in Hartly, look like walking advertisements for the fair even as they stroll the grounds.

Their well-decorated children's safari wagon – bedecked with American flags and rows of colorful pompom chicks from Delmarva Poultry Industry Inc. – carries bags full of various freebies from booths and agencies, along with the occasional snack and souvenir.

"We love coming to the fair – every day, every year," said Donna Ratledge, an irrigation company owner.

"We wouldn't miss the fair, not for anything," her 16-year-old Mary added.

Her mother, who has been coming to the fair as long as she can remember, recalls one year when she went with her pregnant sister – who doesn't like to miss the fair either – but she had to leave the fairgrounds when she went into labor.

Ratledge and her daughter said they enjoyed but miss the youth talent show and livestock birthing center that the fair featured years ago and they hope that the fair might consider bringing back those events in the future. But they understand that it's good for the fair to try new events and attractions, adding that they love the fair and have only positive things to say about it.

Mother: "We love the freebies and the pretty animal contest."

Daughter: "And the demolition derby is something fun to do."

Mother: "Also, we always like the marketplace."

Daughter: "I like the rides – 'Ring of Fire' – the food and the rides."

 Mother: "And I like the livestock."

Daughter: "I like the livestock, too."

Mother: "And we love the 4-H."

Daughter: "Yes, we do."

Mother: "I guess we love everything about the fair, including the variety."

Daughter: "You sure are right, Mom. We sure love the state fair."

IN THE TENTS

Two special fans of the Delaware State Fair say their unique, if somewhat old-fashioned presence here gives them a special opportunity to visit with hundreds, if not thousands of fairgoers each year.

As the snake lady (Cindy Feagin) and the World's Smallest Woman (Linda Nelson) – complete with dramatic, carnival-style painted signs on their tents – the two share an upbeat modern take on being fair attractions along with the likes of the World's Smallest Horse and World's Biggest Tortoise.

And there's nothing freakish about either of them.

Cindy Feagin, a South Carolina native who lives in Florida, has been working this fair for a dozen years and thoroughly enjoys the work. "I wouldn't miss it for the world," she said.

The work isn't too taxing for someone like herself, a sickly 60-year-old who weighs just 80 pounds and suffers from anemia as well as chronic obstructive pulmonary disease, known as COPD.

As Angel the Snake Lady of Borneo, she is the star of a master illusion, said to date from the 16th century.

Those who enter her tent see the figure of a huge snake, described as a 200-pound Burmese python – with her head – on top of a table.

Sometimes the first sight sends terror through her young visitors and some start to run away. Others just stare.

"I tell them, 'Don't be afraid, it's a magic trick,'" she said.

When children ask their most common questions – how she brushes her teeth and drives – she says she is assisted by her pet monkey Freddy and gets rides when she needs to.

Once her guests are relaxed, she hits them with her message.

"I tell them 'Don't do drugs. Stay in school,'" she said. "That's the whole point of the show."

She looks forward to bringing her show and her message to the fair for many years to come.

"I love coming to Delaware," she said. "It's my favorite place of everywhere I go across the country."

Thirty-eight-year-old Linda Nelson, also of Florida, voices similar affection for the fair.

"The people are just so nice here," she said, adding that fair staff members often check on her, bring her cold water and see if she needs anything. "They couldn't be nicer."

So Delaware has become a favorite stop in her national tours stretched over many years with billing as Little Linda, the World's Smallest Woman.

"Some people get scared because they think I'm not real, then I say 'Hello' and start talking to them," Nelson said with a relaxed smile.

After initially being startled, she said, visitors enjoy chatting and many have their pictures taken with her.

The most frequent question she gets is why she is so small.

"I tell them I was born this way," she said.

The two other most-frequent questions are whether she is married – she isn't – and whether she is happy – she is.

She says she enjoys her work because "it helps people see that we're all people, no matter how different we look."

TRANSCENDING TIME

As the Delaware State Fair began a century ago, ours was a vastly different time for the state and nation.

World War I was a recent memory and the state's population – now nearing the million mark – was counted at just 219,000. Movies were becoming popular and more

families were starting to get cars, as assembly-line production lowered the price of Henry Ford's Model-T to less than $500. Woodrow Wilson was serving as the nation's 28th president, Selbyville's John G. Townsend Jr. was Delaware's governor and the end of Prohibition was more than a decade in the future.

But the fair at Harrington already was starting to create an enduring legacy that would be both handed down and experienced anew as generation after generation shared in the fair's excitement, exhibits, entertainment, attractions, food and fun.

And while changing eras have framed the fair, reactions of those who attend – shown in the faces photographed and shared decade after decade – seem to transcend their times and time itself. On that theme, throughout this book, we share images selected by Danny Aguilar, the fair's assistant general manager and director of marketing.

FACES BEHIND THE FAIR

DAVID G. JONES is an icon of dedication and devotion to the Delaware State Fair, a familiar face behind-the-scenes. At 83 years old, he proudly says, "I missed two years while I was in the Army, but that's the only time I missed the fair."

But nearly 40 years ago, the experience for this longtime fair director grew suddenly deeper – and became a duo – thanks to a love-match that began with a blind date at the fair.

"I met him on a blind date," said Diana Jones, his wife of three dozen years and a Delaware State Fair stalwart in her own right.

On the day of their first date, she remembers liking his suggestion that they go to the Harrington fair and accepted his invitation. She knew he was a fair director – and soon learned what that entailed.

She had no idea that, once they got to the fair, her husband-to-be would put her right into the swing of things – getting her to pitch in.

But he did.

"So I worked all 10 days," she said with a smile. "And I have ever since."

She, too, has become a longtime supporter and one of the friendliest faces behind the fair. She spends much of her fair time managing the VIP Lounge, working with volunteers – including her granddaughter – serving up hearty lunches to judges, officials, media personnel and other guests.

Above: Diana Jones and David G. Jones
On facing page: Harvey Kenton in carriage, Fair Director Dave Wilson driving

The Joneses have been involved in many aspects of the fair, including as sponsors of the tasty Chocolate Temptation Competition in the Culinary Department, supplying cash prizes for winners of the contest that ends with sharing delicious entries.

Diana also started a simple way to make guests' VIP Lounge lunches help others.

She collects tabs from their canned beverages to donate to Ronald McDonald House. The charity recycles the high-grade aluminum tabs – more valuable and easier to store than whole cans – and uses the money to help fund free housing for families of critically ill children visiting the area for medical care.

"Every little tab helps," she said.

As one guest dropped her tab into the jar and promised to return to the fair with more, Dave Jones popped by.

"Just checking if you need anything," he said.

"No," his wife replied. "We're in good shape."

When she turned to serve a dessert, he watched her, eyes twinkling. "She's just wonderful," he told a nearby guest in a gruff whisper. "Don't tell her, but I know what a lucky man I am."

And so is the Delaware State Fair to have folks such as the two of them, sharing generations of dedication among the faces behind the fair.

Right, from left: Jeanie DeLeo, William Jester, Ron Hatfield, Dennis Hazzard, LeRoy Betts and Harvey Kenton

THE TEA LADY

Diana Chaney was volunteering one day at the fair when a fairgoer mentioned to how nice it is that people like her give their time every year to help make the fair a success.

"I love being part of the fair," Chaney said. "The people are just wonderful."

She and other volunteers don't think of what they do to help the fair as "work," she said, adding,

"We all believe in the fair and we have fun here."

A while ago, she volunteered with The Grange, she said, and that was how her grandmother-in-law set the standard for her family's tradition of helping out at the fair.

Sally Chaney of Bridgeville always volunteered at The Grange and always served tea, her granddaughter-in-law said.

"Every year, she came and camped out at the back of the Grange Hall – all week," she added. "She made so many cakes at home and at The Grange. She kept volunteering even when she was in her 70s and 80s and she was always known as 'The Tea Lady.'"

Left: Rebekkah Conley, left, and Trish Dunlap
Right: Danny Aguilar and crowd

KEY TO SUCCESS

Although they work largely behind the scenes, the fair's volunteers are known as its not-so-secret weapon, as well as the secret to its success.

That dedicated cadre has been cited as a key to the fair's longevity, setting it apart from other fairs that that have come and gone in Delaware since the 1800s.

"The Fair's success can probably be attributed to the myriads of people over the years to whom the Fair has been a very important institution and who have donated countless hours on its behalf," University of Delaware history researcher Saralee Webb Towers wrote in her 1984 paper, "The History of Agricultural Fairs in Delaware."

The volunteers from all walks of life – whose efforts from organization to grounds-keeping have been, literally, priceless – are deeply appreciated. Hundreds of volunteers help each year, from high school students doing community service to doting grandparents who remember attending the fair when they were children and want to help younger generations have equally wonderful memories to treasure.

The fair actually conducted a study to gain insight into volunteers' contributions to the 10-day event. The study, conducted in 2009, found that that year's fair involved a whopping 40,000 volunteer hours.

"I can tell you this for sure, that if it wasn't for our volunteers, there wouldn't be a Delaware State Fair," General Manager Bill DiMondi said. "We couldn't do this without them."

Right, from left: Dennis Hazzard, Ron Hatfield, Ronald Cowdrick, Dave Merrifield,,Ken Andrejak, and Randy Hooker

Left:: Jack Short and youth competitor

LEGACY OF LEADERSHIP

Over slightly more than a century, a steady flow of caring citizens have devoted their time, talent and energy to the fair and its success.

Literally thousands have served in leadership positions with responsibilities that have evolved as the decades have passed.

In noting presidents and general managers here, we honor all who served with them in the important roles of vice president, treasurer, secretary and Executive Committee.

FAIR PRESIDENTS

Charles D. Murphy Sr.
1920-1928

Benjamin I. Shaw
1929-1947

Jacob O. Williams
1948-1958

J. Gordon Smith
1959-1975

Robert F. Rider
1976-1988

William M. Chambers Jr.
1988-1996

William J. DiMondi
1996-2008

W. LeRoy Betts
2008-2011

R. Ronald Draper
2011-present

Top, from left, LeRoy Betts, Bill DiMondi, Bill Chambers, Bob Rider Sr.
Bottom, from left: George Scuse, Bill DiMondi, Dennis Hazzard

FAIR MANAGERS

When the Delaware State Fair began, day-to-day matters were handled by Ernest Raughley, who served decades as the organization's secretary. Following his death in 1948, the organization created the position of general manager, filling the post for the first time the next year.

Ernest Raughley
1919-1948

T. Brinton Holloway
1949-1961

George C. Simpson
1961-1985

F. Gary Simpson
1985-1992

Dennis S. Hazzard
1992-2007

William J. DiMondi
2008-present

Left, in red: Fair Director Michael Wasylkowski
Right, from left: Director Dave Wilson, President Ron Draper, Vice President Harvey Kenton

UNPAID STALWARTS

Since its start in 1919, the Delaware State Fair Board of Directors has grown from 39 to 80 members – all holders of the fair's no-dividend stock – who represent all three counties of the state and serve without pay as they devote time and energy year-round to the planning, hosting and growth of the annual event. The entire board of 80 members stands annually for election by the shareholders.

Board members serve on one or more of the 21 standing committees, whose chairs serve on the executive board along with the seven officers, plus four directors elected by the board and two directors appointed by the president. The board also has honorary members, elected after their long and meritorious service to the fair.

Over the past century, uncounted hundreds of directors have contributed to building the Delaware State Fair to its current success.

Early days' directors also are honored for having donated their time and energy to do much of the work now done by fair employees and contractors, from trash patrol to track preparations.

Although it is impossible to name every one of them here, past directors' vital roles and personal dedication cannot be overstated. This recognition of the current Board of Directors, going into the centennial, also is intended to express gratitude and pay tribute to all directors who previously served.

CURRENT BOARD OF DIRECTORS

Brent M. Adams Jr.

J. William Andrew

Eugene H. Bayard

W. LeRoy Betts

R. Bruce Betts

Mark Breeding

Ronald Breeding

Harold K. Brode

Donald Bullock

Josef A. Burger

Arthur B. Cahall III

L. Aaron Chaffinch

Jeff Chambers

Hon. Kenneth S. Clark Jr. (1st VP)

Allen J. Cook

Kristin Cook

William J. Cook

C. Douglas Crouse (Treasurer)

John M. Curtis Jr.

Jeanie DeLeo (3rd VP)

A. Eugene Dill

William J. DiMondi (Secretary)

R. Ronald Draper (President)

Jason Hall

Marian Handlin

Ron Hatfield

John W. Hendricks

John W. Hickey

Robert A. Holloway

John D. Hukill

Karen Hutchison

Ronald W. Jarrell

William G. Jester

Amy Jones

David G. Jones

Ruthi Adams Joseph

Hon. Harvey Kenton (2nd VP)

Robert Killen

Todd F. Lawson

George Luff

Roger Marino

Kenneth L. McDowell

Donald R. McLamb Jr.

James W. Messick

James W. Messick Jr.

Anne T. Minner

G. Robert Moore Jr.

Elizabeth "Betsy" Morris

Donna Mowbray

Nikki Mowbray

Russ Neal

Hon. William R. Outten

Coulter Passwaters

Pete Pizzadili

Robert E. Price

Harry E. Raughley

Anthony Richardson

Robert F. Rider Jr.

Richard L. Sapp Sr.

James M. Satterfield

James M. Satterfield IV

Michael Scuse

Denis Shaffer

Hon. F. Gary Simpson

Shelly Winkler Simpson

Brian Somers

Robert Taylor

Dr. H. Wesley Towers Jr.

Susan Truehart-Garey

Deborah Vanderwende

Jesse Vanderwende

William Vanderwende

Jimmy Warren

Peni Warren

Michael Wasylkowski

Elaine Webb

N. Edgar Welch

Hon. David L. Wilson

EXECUTIVE BOARD

J. William Andrew

W. LeRoy Betts

Mark Breeding

Josef A. Burger

Hon. Kenneth S. Clark Jr.

C. Douglas Crouse

Jeanie DeLeo

A. Eugene Dill

William J. DiMondi

R. Ronald Draper

Ronald Hatfield

Robert A. Holloway

Amy Jones

Hon. Harvey R. Kenton Jr.

Donald R. McLamb Jr.

James W. Messick

G. Robert Moore

Harry E. Raughley

F. Gary Simpson

Peni Warren

HONORARY DIRECTORS

Delbert Cain

Richard Calhoun

James L. Crothers

Mary Pitlick

Robert E. Taylor

David Woodward

Top left, from left: Jimmy Warren, Russ Neal

Top right, from left: Director Jimmy Messick, II, fair employee Kenny Baird, Director Jimmy Messick, fair employee John Murphy

Bottom left, from left: Thurman Adams, his wife Hilda Adams, Bill Chambers, Betty Chambers

Bottom right, back row from left: Amanda Rockemann, Erica VanVessen, Kate Brown, Jacob Dunlap; in front, Robin Rockemann, Rentals and Concessions Manager

Top right: Unidentified, Director Amy Jones
Center left: Robert A. Taylor
Center right: Bonnie Kendall, Judy Glasco
Bottom left: Director Anne Minner

Top, from left: Ken Clark, Harvey Kenton, Jeanie DeLeo, Bill Vanderwende, Ron Draper, Michael Scuse (in hat), Doug Crouse and Bill DiMondi
Center left: Bob Moore, Director and Livestock Superintendent
Bottom right: Helen Maloney
Bottom left: LeRoy Betts

Top: Bill DiMondi and Patti Key, CEO of Harrington Raceway & Casino

Bottom right: Ali Bishop, Kaylee Collison, Tessa MacDonald, Danny Aguilar, Sara Sipple

Bottom left: Bill DiMondi and long-time fair employee Neal Quail

FROM THE DIRECTORS

In the spirit of the 100th anniversary of the Delaware State Fair, all current members of the organization's board of directors were invited to provide any comment they might want to share – 100 words or less – for inclusion in this commemorative book honoring the fair's past and looking to its future. Here now, in alphabetical order, are thoughts from Delaware State Fair's directors.

Mark A. Breeding of Felton
Director since 2014
Agricultural Education/FFA Department Superintendent

100 years of highlighting the best of Delaware Agriculture, family fun, anticipation and excitement for exhibitors, providing countless memories and traditions for all. This is what I believe the Delaware State Fair has given to our great State.

Ron Breeding of Greenwood
Director since 2000

Having grown up about 5 miles from the Fair, I attended it for over 60 years. I have seen many changes during those years. My parents would pack a picnic lunch and take us to watch Strates unload their train along with all their rides and games wagons. It was just like the circus coming to town.

As I grew up, I entered 4-H exhibits. This was something I looked forward every year winning the ribbons. Then I exhibited animals. There were so many lessons learned working with them. I think I chased more hogs and cows than I showed.

Buck Cahall
Director since 1984

What does the Delaware State Fair mean to me?

As a kid, the animals were great, the Midway rides, seeing Pat Boone in person, great food! As a teenager, seeing Rock and Roll shows, the Joie Chitwood Show, wanting to go to the "Girly Show" .... (didn't). And those rides!

Above: Nick Fedurko of AAA Communications

As a Dad, loving it when my kids could hardly wait for Fairtime and the same things I could hardly wait for. Seeing their excitement at New Kids, Milli Vanilli, Miami Sound Machine and others!!!

As a Director, helping make sure this great event called the Delaware State Fair carries on for another 100 years of Tradition and Family Fun!!!

L. Aaron Chaffinch of the Bridgeville area
Director since 2001

As a young lad, I attended the Delaware State Fair yearly as a 4-Her. I have very fond memories of each year entering my vegetables from my garden project. Additionally, I think back to the countless hours working on a window display with my fellow 4-Hers. Our window display, which was from the local Dublin Hill Yellow Jackets 4-H Club, won first place at the fair on a state level. The theme of our winning display was "4-H Builds Better Citizens." My best guess would be the fair of 1968. Back then, interacting at the fair with 4-Hers from all over the state of Delaware, was a **super** experience.

Kristin Cook of Camden
Director since 2007

Delaware State fair is held near and dear to my heart. The Fair is a time for friends and family to come together, to rekindle friendships, to laugh and love, to celebrate hard work and achievement, and to cheer others on. The fair is a special place where magic happens, and I believe everyone is better for having visited. There are many life lessons learned by being involved in all the aspects that the fair encompasses.

Jeanie Thomas DeLeo of Dover
Director since 2008

Having grown up in Harrington, belonging to a family deeply involved with the Fair, it naturally runs through my veins! Even as the Fair has grown and evolved over these past 100 years – thanks to the vision, dedication and hard work of all the involved volunteers, employees, staff, shareholders, vendors, exhibitors, attendees and Directors – its roots have remained firmly planted in providing an educational, competitive, entertaining, wholesome venue for all ages to enjoy! The Fair for me is a place of great excitement and energy, heritage and memories, yearly awaited re-connections, traditions, new experiences, and always a variety of great food!! I am proud and humbled to serve in some small way as a Director of this wonderful

Above: Paul Chandler, retired fair electrician

organization! I feel the Delaware State Fair is a bright, shining star for the great State of Delaware!! Happy 100th Anniversary!! Here's to many more!

Ron Hatfield of Portsville
Director since 1989

Fondest memories

It is so exciting and fabulous that we are celebrating the 100th Anniversary of the Fair and I have so many wonderful memories, from when I was a young boy to present day.

One of them would be, from the early 1950s, as a young boy & teen. I would sell programs in the grandstands for 10 cents each, of which I would get to keep a penny for each one sold. During this time, a penny was a lot of money.

But I must say, my fondest memories are from and with my friends, family and the many people I have met over the many years. Too many to name. And I cherish every one of them. We all became one big family, the "Harrington Fair Family."

The spirit of the fair lives on, through all of us.

Congratulations Everyone!

Harvey Kenton of Milford
Director Since 1986

I think it was 1985 when I joined the board. I was handed a share of stock by Franklin Hendricks and one from Walter Messick and they said, welcome to the board of the Delaware State Fair. What an honor. Now a Vice President of the Fair. So proud of our Fair. As a youth I never missed a Fair and I haven't missed a day in the last 33 years. Every day, I walk through the livestock barns and through all the buildings. The people are wonderful. I think we have one of the top Fairs in the nation and I'm proud to be a part of it.

Todd F. Lawson of Harbeson
Director since 2017

Four generations of my family have participated in the "Harrington Fair," as we grew up calling it. I have fond memories of driving to the Fair and getting so excited to see this huge event as we drove up the highway. As I grew older, my brother and I showed animals and met life-long friends while camping at the Fair. Now, I am proud to say my children and my brother's children are all growing up with the Fair and showing their own animals. The Fair provides this unique and priceless experience that I will forever cherish.

G. Robert Moore Jr. of Harrington
Director since 1975

The Delaware State Fair has always meant showing Dairy Cattle. I started exhibiting my Ayrshire Dairy Cattle in 1962. My daughters showed and now my Granddaughter shows. We had our first Grand Champion in 1966. I remember Andy Burger, a fellow exhibitor, needed another animal to make up a group class. I loaned him one of mine and his group beat mine in the class. He was happy and on that show day we became the best of friends. We have many great friendships that were formed at the Fair.

One special happening is that my daughter and now my son-in-law of 25 years relationship started at the Fair. My daughter Laurie and her cow Velvet were the first to enter the new Simpson Show Barn. As we move on to the more recent years, my Granddaughter's heifer was the Futurity winner, as well as, the Supreme Heifer in both the Open and Junior Shows.

My wife and I and our entire family still look forward to the Fair even more that we did when we were all younger. I remember the old barns and grounds, but I am so proud of the beautiful facility and have today. 100 years of a great tradition.

Betsy Morris of Newark
Director Since 1998

University of Delaware Extension Educator, 4-H

The state fair has been a Cook/Morris family tradition for five generations. My fond memory is as a child leaving our dairy farm in Newark to head to the fair. We piled into the station wagon with at least one pull-over necessary to stop sibling bickering. As the excitement was building it culminated with a yell of "STATE FAIR" when the water tower came into sight. It meant we were almost there! I still shout "STATE FAIR" (in my head) when I see the water tower each year.

Gene Price of Harrington
Director since 2005

I am very proud of what the Delaware State Fair has become. It is an asset to Harrington and our entire State with activities going on all year long! Congratulations to all the current directors, Management and Staff, and all those who served over these hundred years, I know they would be proud!

Jim Satterfield III of Wyoming
Director since 1987

Jim Satterfield IV of Wyoming
Director since 2013

Our fondest memories of the Fair center around spending time with friends and family. There is a special Fair fraternity made up of a number of folks you may only see once a year at Fair time. Spending time catching up with them is priceless. Serving on the Board of Directors has also been a cherished memory. Making new friendships and working side by side with others who share the common goal of growing and caring for the Fair has been an amazing experience!

F. Gary Simpson of Dover
Director since 1985

My Fair memory starts when I was about 6 years old and I showed my first calf. My older brothers and cousins had been showing for years. Unlike my brothers, I wasn't old enough to sleep in the barn. What a thrill when I was older and finally allowed to spend the entire week there. After restless nights sleeping on scratchy straw, and eating lots of junk food during the day, I was happy to get back home when the Fair ended in order to get a good night sleep and eat my mom's good cooking... at least until next year's Fair, when I couldn't wait to do it all over again!

Shelly Winkler Simpson of Houston
Beef Cattle Superintendent
Director since 2018

Some of my favorite Fair memories are with my dad and my grandparents showing cattle. My dad began showing beef cattle around age 12 and had to ask special permission to exhibit Polled Herefords. My brother and I continued to show beef cattle and our grandparents enjoyed watching us show and supporting us in all of our Fair projects. My grandfather was especially proud of the numerous Grand and Reserve champion banners we won with our market steers. My husband and I met at the Delaware State Fair and on July 24, 2019, we will celebrate our twentieth wedding anniversary, at the Fair. Our children, Brooke, Kathryn and Travis, continue our tradition of showing cattle. The Fair is like our family vacation and each year I enjoy the time we spend together and the memories we are making.

Rob Taylor of Harrington
Director since 2014

The Delaware State Fair has been a part of my life for as long as I can remember from running on the dirt midway to patronizing all the iconic vendors past and present. But the best part is watching people gather and talking, some not seeing each other in months and others just seeing them the night before. I always look forward to the fair coming but also know that once the fair is over to me, Summer is over and can't wait 'til next year. Congratulations to the Delaware State Fair for 100 years and to hundreds more!

Elaine Z. Webb of Greenwood
Kent County 4-H Leader
Director since 2013

4-Hers spend hundreds of hours throughout the year preparing for the 10 days of Fair. At the Fair, 4-Hers showcase the time and dedication they have devoted to each of their projects, from the bluebird box constructed in September, to the speech prepared in January, to the market animal project they cared for throughout the spring and summer. 4-Hers' interests are as varied as the members themselves but they are all bound together in their love for the Fair. They love the competition and the 4-H camaraderie that makes the best better.

Senator David Wilson of Lincoln
Director since 2000

Attending and participating in the Delaware State Fair is something I look forward to every summer. My fondest memories include showing horses with my son and serving with Clarence Scuse and Jim Crothers. Over the years my involvement with the Fair has increased. After assuming a Directorship in 2000, I have served on the Entertainment Committee and recently took on the responsibility of Superintendent of the Horse and Pony Department. The Fair has changed greatly over the years, but the one thing that remains the same is the comradery, excitement and commitment of countless volunteers determined to make each Fair experience a success.

The Fair brings families together, creates friendships and allows visitors and participants alike the opportunity to enjoy quality entertainment, the thrill of the midway attractions, good food, friendly competition in the show ring plus much more. But I am most impressed and inspired by the young people and their interest in agriculture and their dedication to the Fair. They will be the ones that ensure the continuation of the legacy of the Delaware State Fair for the next 100 years.

Above: Honorary Director Mary Pitlick

EARLY APPRECIATION

An editorial published by the Every Evening on the eve of the 1931 fair's opening provides insight into how the relatively young event was faring in public opinion at the time and how those who organized it were regarded.

Perhaps most notable, however, is that the editorial represented the position of the Wilmington-based newspaper, praising the fair, in part, for being an effective statewide meeting ground.

KENT AND SUSSEX FAIR

Experience has proved that the heart of the rural section is the logical place for a state fair in Delaware. Wilmington, which has half of the State's population, Dover, Middletown and other towns have had fairs. None of these survived. The only one that seems to have successfully passed the experimental stage and to have given evidence of ability to be self sustaining, is the one at Harrington, known as the Kent and Sussex Fair.

It is not very old – only a few years – but so far has proved a success. And while it bears the name "Kent and Sussex," it is recognized as a statewide institution. Wilmington and the rest of New Castle County contribute their share toward the patronage. That is where our people meet on common ground with those of Kent and Sussex....

Entrenched as the fair is, in the good graces of the public, the undertaking is encouraged to do "just a little better" in the matter of attractions each year. In addition to keeping up the plant on the grounds at all times, usually a building or two is added each year. So, when the fair opens its gates tomorrow for this year's exhibition, everything will be found in good shape and adequate to meet the requirements of the exhibitors and patrons.

The program is mapped out for the remainder of the week, which is said to include the best racing list there yet, insures success, if the weather is favorable – and it generally is during the "week of the Harrington fair," as residents in that part of the State will testify.

Those who are responsible for the Harrington fair are to be commended not only for the sacrifice of their own time many of them make, but also for their excellent judgment in making it a worthwhile exhibition.

They doubtless realize how badly off the State would be without a fair and they are doing what they can to assure its continuance.

FROM THE FARM

ANYONE WHO ARRIVES early any day of the Delaware State Fair can find Harvey Kenton without much trouble.

"I'll be in the animal barns – all of them," he said.

"I don't have a favorite, but I walk through all of them every day."

And a good morning might see him starting that morning walk with a scrapple sandwich for breakfast.

Kenton, who has served 32 years on the fair board, announced his retirement from the Delaware Legislature. But he's not retiring from the fair. "Not so long as I can breathe and walk," he added with a chuckle.

He plans to spend his "extra time" taking agricultural business management classes, continuing the interest in farming he has had since childhood.

Even in modern times as the state fair marks a century of operation, agriculture – the business that got it started – remains Delaware's top industry, accounting for nearly 40 percent of land in the state.

In the state where the modern chicken industry began and continues to support close to 14,000 jobs, broilers are the top commodity, with Sussex County still ranking as the nation's top producer at 200+ million birds a year.

The fair is a prime opportunity for that community to increase public understanding, said James Fisher, communications manager for the 1,800-member Delmarva Poultry Industry Inc. trade association.

The main question people ask helps him dispel a widespread lack of understanding, Fisher said. "The big misconception is that we still use hormones and steroids, but they've been illegal since the 1950s – full stop," he said.

At the association's display – near tables with information on agricultural topics from forestry to soybeans – children answered basic questions about eggs and chickens to win prizes such as fuzzy pom-pom chicks and mint candies.

Many parents, meanwhile, collected recipe cards from a variety of agencies and companies, focusing on Delaware-produced crops, also well-represented in open and youth competition categories.

Kenton said he enjoys visiting with all the agricultural exhibitors, regardless of their age or their classes of competition.

He and others note that the fair's Junior Livestock Auction is a highlight for young exhibitors, although after a year of tending the animals, their sale can be a tearful time. In an exciting auction for the fair's 99th year, more than 100 of the youngsters'

top-winning livestock made a strong showing as they sold for a total of nearly $200,000.

Kenton, who has a lot of fond fair memories from his 4-H Club youth in Milford said that, looking back, has only one regret: "I wish I'd saved my ribbons."

As an adult, he also got involved in FFA, including as a national judge.

The opportunity for families, especially children, to see a wide variety of animals is an important and integral part of the Delaware State Fair, he and others say.

"I've been exhibiting 45 years," said Cheryl Vest of Clayton, as giant fans blew cool breezes through rows of cow stalls.

"The best part, I find, is educating the public about where their meat, milk and eggs come from," said Vest, who also teaches at Middletown High School.

In modern times, children may grow up never having seen a farm, never understanding all the hard work people put into producing the food they eat, she said.

For fairgoers to see what farms produce up close and talk to people who devote their lives to them is "probably the most important impact we can have," she said.

Agricultural craft demonstrations and farm equipment – from the Antique Machinery Showcase to distributors' ultra-modern, computer-controlled giants – also dazzle fairgoers ranging from multi-generational agriculture families to flowerbox gardeners.

Although unseen by those who attend the fair, state animal health inspectors each year check the more than 3,000 animals before they compete.

Livestock shows and pull competitions for tractors and horses always draw big crowds, but for small-scale encounters of the agricultural kind, nothing beats Allen Harim's interactive display full of fuzzy chicks.

For Sue Bump of Dover, it's the beauty of the beasts that draws her back to the fair, year after year.

"I come down and take pictures of the horse shows," she said.

Over the years, she added, the animals have become her favorite part of the fair.

"When I was a kid, it was the rides, but I'm 45 now," she said.

Ron Breeding, a longtime fair director and leader, recalls one recent encounter that he shares as an example of how significantly educational the fair can be.

His earlier memories of the fair date from growing up on a dairy farm as a young 4-Her in the Andrewsville Speedies 4-H Club. In those days, his mother would pack a picnic and they would go to the fair every night – partly to see people they hadn't seen since the previous fair – and eat while

sitting outside the old administration building, replaced many years ago.

The fair was a big part of his 20 years as a 4-H Club leader, with his wife Sue, and decades showing beef cows with their boys. Back then, he recalled, most of the folks he knew had a pretty good understanding of farming and agriculture.

But the educational encounter took him aback and made him realize that, the farther people become removed from the sources of their food, the more they have to learn.

The encounter began as he saw a young mother showing her kids some of the fair's produce entries.

She came upon the peas and stopped.

"She had no idea what they were," Breeding said. "So I opened a pod and showed her the peas."

As it turned out, the woman was as amazed as her children were. Before that, she had only seen peas come out of a can or a freezer bag, he said.

"So you can see," he added, "that we're encouraging agriculture and educating the public – and not just kids."

The fair's agricultural evolution and continuing emphasis on farms – 99 percent of which are family-owned statewide – were aptly observed by News Journal reporter Jeff Montgomery.

"While the poultry industry and its crop needs dominate Delaware's farm economy, family farm traditions and priorities dominate the fair's livestock, poultry and other competitive exhibits," Montgomery wrote in 2015.

And as educating the public about farm life and food production has become an increasing priority for exhibiting families, he noted that the fair has become "Delaware's celebration of a state culture and industry that has become a mix of high-tech business and home-centered enterprise."

POPULAR POULTRY

Newcomers to the fair, including first-time visitors to the fair's Poultry Barn tend to ask just how chickens got to be such a big deal here in Delaware.

But that's kind of a trick question because it requires two distinctly separate answers.

FIRST, BLUE HENS

The state bird is the legendary and extinct Blue Hen Chicken, made famous during the Revolutionary War. The game birds, said to be a steely blue, were carried by soldiers in Captain Jonathan Caldwell's company from Kent County.

The birds were said to be so scrappy in troops' recreational cockfights – now illegal – that the state's scrappy soldiers were nicknamed after them.

The birds, said to be from a particular brood but not a true breed of their own, went extinct but many have tried to breed other chickens to claim the Blue Hen title, shared by University of Delaware's cartoon mascot.

SECOND, A LUCKY MISTAKE

The modern reason that chickens are such big business in Delaware is that the whole poultry industry got its start here.

Thanks to the late Cecile Steele of Ocean View.

In 1923, she ordered 50 chicks for a home flock, but the hatchery sent 500 by mistake.

From left: Lieutenant Governor Bethany Hall-Long, Governor John Carney

Livestock Judging - Delaware State Fair - 1928

Steele, who mainly wanted chickens for eggs, raised the excess chickens, sold them by the pound to buyers throughout the region. She ordered 1,000 chicks the next year and repeated the process.

The idea caught on, as chicken gained popularity on the menus of restaurants and hotels, creating big demand well before broiler chickens would become a grocery store staple.

And in less than a decade, there were about 500 other Delawareans growing broiler chickens.

Although the industry spread far and wide, its Sussex County birthplace still has bragging rights for the highest per capita concentration of chickens found anywhere in the country.

And poultry industry leaders say the Delaware State Fair is the very best place to see them at their absolute, blue-ribbon finest.

FUN FARM FACTS

With agriculture as its No. 1 industry, Delaware also leads the nation in the value of the agricultural products produced from every acre.

That's just one of the "Cool Delaware Agriculture Facts" that the state Department of Agriculture shares, drawing on its own statistics as well as information from the U.S. Department of Agriculture and the University of Delaware.

- 30,000 people work in agriculture and forestry in Delaware
- Delaware has 508,652 acres or 41 percent of the land total in farming
- 99 percent of Delaware's farms are family-owned
- We have 2,451 farms or one for every 378 people in our state
- More than half the state's family farms have less than 50 acres
- Our farmers harvest 9,500 acres of lima beans, more than any other state
- More than 700 Delaware farms have horses and ponies

- There are more than 6,000 horses and ponies on farms in the state

- Nearly 700 family farms raise First State chickens

- Nearly 80 family farms in the state raise cows for milk

- 40 of our family farms grow strawberries

- Our farmers grow about 11,000 acres of sweet corn

- Watermelons are grown on about 2,500 acres in the state

- More than 15 Delaware farms grow apples

- More than 1 of every 4 acres of Delaware farmland is permanently preserved

- It takes 300 million honeybees to pollinate crops in the state

The Delaware Department of Agriculture also inspects the livestock before Delaware State Fair competition, educates thousands of elementary school students about fire safety each year, inspects about 500 businesses for harmful plant pests and diseases and certify more than 3,750 pesticide applicators each year.

Agency inspectors annually check the accuracy of more than 10,000 gas pumps statewide. Learn more about Delaware agriculture at agriculture.delaware.gov.

EXTRAORDINARY EATS

ANTWON TRIMBALL, an educator from Laurel, had no doubt: "My favorite part of the fair would, absolutely, have to be the food."

"I love the chicken and I've tried the big [smoked] turkey legs, but I'm not too big on trying what's new."

Classics endure on the Harrington grounds, where popcorn, hotdogs, roasted nuts and cotton candy still provide the old-fashioned fair flavor, with an assortment of modern interpretations.

Fried fare, said to have begun with French fries, long ago added options from onion rings to funnel cakes.

But in recent years, there's been a famous Delaware State Fair saying that, "If you can fry it, you can find it here."

And that goes far beyond fried green tomatoes, corn dogs, breaded mushrooms and blooming onions.

The first big fry variation appears to have been deep-fried Twinkies, closely followed by such now-classics as deep-fried ice cream, Oreos, Snickers bars, pickles and tacos.

Adventurous fair fans every year scour the fair's 75+ food vendors, on a mission to discover something new, special and perhaps challenging to eat.

Among the oddest of most-recent additions from the world of food fads: Cappuccino or espresso served in chocolate-lined waffle-style ice cream cones.

And then there were deep-fried tacos and lobster macaroni-and-cheese, making smash-hit debuts at the 99th annual fair. But the same fair – like many preceding it – saw ample takers for classics eats from pizza slices and Spaghetti Eddie dinners to chicken or ham platters made by volunteers of the Delaware State Grange, "Moose ears" by the Harrington Moose Lodge and the Greenwood Mennonite School's barbecue chicken with roasted corn that keep crowds coming back year after year.

With a balance of local and out-of-town food vendors, another classic is Harrington's own Kirby and Holloway. The super-local stand, a fair fixture of decades from the company formed in 1947, boasts the "No. 1 Sausage at the Delaware State Fair." But it's also a go-to for scrapple sandwiches.

The fair's fun food reputation does not go unnoticed by the media.

Many local media have highlighted fair vendors' shark kebobs and alligator bites at Chester's Gators & Taters, and scorpion- and insect-topped pies at Swain's Pizza on a Stick – both included in recent years' News Journal coverage of the growing availability of healthy food options at the fair, along with salads and kabobs at Demitri's Fine Fresh Greek Food.

TV's Cooking Channel made the fair's food even more famous through its popular "Carnival Eats" series that airs throughout North America.

Two episodes of the show's 2017 season prominently featured Delaware State Fair's come-and-get-it comestibles unlikely to be found many places across the country – but continuing to dazzle viewers in reruns.

Host Noah Cappe's first show about the fair initially aired on May 5, 2017, and featured him eating "the very stately Delaware Dog," loaded with scrapple. He then tackled a Frankenfunnel Burger, a stacked burger with a funnel cake in the middle. Next was the Octotaco, loaded with octopus, followed by the Killer Cereal Treat, one of many deep-fried oddities available at the fair, this one with fruity breakfast cereal hot from the fryer and smothered with ice cream.

The second episode highlighting the fair aired that June 30. Promotions boasted that "Host Noah Cappe knows Dela-where to find amazing fresh seafood, the Delaware State Fair in Harrington."

In that episode, he started with a Shrimp Dog, which is like a corndog, but with corn-battered shrimp, then

indulged in a Crabtastic Po'Boy stuffed with a whole soft-shell crab. He then went Delaware-classic with an apple-scrapple burger and finished on a sweet note with a beer-battered and deep-fried slice of Key Lime Pie.

The show's national attention has been a boon for food vendors at the fair.

After seeing their trademark dishes on that show, Sea Hogg Street Eats & Catering of Rehoboth Beach became one of the fair vendors with signs that proudly boast, "AS SEEN ON CARNIVAL EATS."

A lot of customers recognize the show name and are drawn to the food truck, its crew said.

One curious foodie even drove more than five hours to the fair, just to try an Octotaco – the octopus-stuffed taco. And he enjoyed it so much, he promised to come back for more.

But fairgoers planning to feast on Sea Hogg's fried frog legs are well-advised to make it snappy if they want that food to make them happy.

That's because Sea Hogg owners Chris and Anthony Jacona use only fresh – not frozen – frog legs, the $10-a-serving summer sensation seems to sell out quickly.

FEEDING FRENZY

Opening day of the fair does more than create big buzz.

It also creates a media feeding frenzy.

"What's the new attraction? Everyone wants to know," said Justina Coronel, a reporter for WMDT 47 ABC of Salisbury, Maryland. "We've done lots of years of live broadcasts."

So have other television stations, web sites and radio stations.

And they also get plenty of company from the Delmarva Peninsula's various newspapers and magazines.

Of course, fairgoers love when their teams hand out prizes and most are willing to put their fun on pause for a brief interview about what they like best or what keeps them coming back to the fair.

Sometimes a new ride like Mega-Drop catches everyone's attention. Or sometimes it's a new fair feature, like The Roost opening with adult beverages. Or there's a special event like the Craft Beer Festival with multiple rock bands that's got folks talking.

You never know exactly what the latest fair buzz will be.

But you can count on the media to search out the newest in fair food.

Coronel and anchor Julian Sadur had so much fun highlighting the fair's wild foods, they started a series called Foodie Fridays. "It's our third year in a row," he said, as they set up for a shoot by Chester's Gators & Taters.

They and a few folks they interviewed agreed that deep-fried tacos and burritos – dunked in beer batter before flash-frying – were both delicious and creative.

And the WDMT team wanted to be the first to tell their viewers and website readers so, because there's always plenty of competition among the media's roving teams that work the fair.

"You'll see the other TV stations," Sadur said, "and you always try to one-up them."

But he and Coronel agree that the one thing any news organization in the region doesn't want to do is ignore the state fair.

"People live for this," Coronel said.

Sadur added, "It's the best thing in Delaware."

INSIDERS' FAVORITES

Mouth-watering aromas filled the room, where tables were laden with some of the wildest and most-classic treats available at the Delaware State Fair.

As the 99th Annual Delaware State Fair entered its final hours, the elaborate smorgasbord was created as a special way to thank staff members for their above-and-beyond work in making the fair a success, General Manager Bill DiMondi said.

Rentals & Concessions Manager Robin Rockemann and her team fanned out over the fairgrounds that afternoon, with Natalie Osorio serving as "master buyer" for the eclectic eats, assisted by Erika VanVessen, Katelynn Brown, Jake Dunlap and Amanda Rockemann.

They assembled the impressive spread that sampled suggestions from staff members and answered the perennial question of what Delaware State Fair insiders most like to eat.

But one staff guest, who said he needed to remain anonymous so he would not be accused of gluttony, confessed that it's almost impossible for fair folks to pick out their favorite foods. "We actually love – and eat – all the food at the fair," he confided in a hushed voice. "Popcorn to frog legs!"

Another quipped, "I think I'm eating everything."

And with that, the staff crew and a few guests made happy, short work of the selections.

"Everyone loves deep fried tacos," said Osorio, who picked up the beef and chicken versions from Jim's.

Nearby were pork nachos, sweet and spicy, from Smoke, Rattle & Roll; quesadillas from Joey's Mexican/K&R Concessions and – a favorite newcomer of 2018 – "Chompers," deep-fried pop-in-your-mouth balls of chicken parmigiana, bacon cheeseburger and taco flavors.

Equally popular were potato nachos from Demetri's, with bacon and jalapenos on the side, and a pair of classics – Perkins' pizza and German bratwurst from Haas's of Dover.

For some in the room, fried pickles from Outlaw Fries were a first-time taste sensation, while many indulged in the fine familiarity of Henry's Kettle Korn from the vendor of the same name.

In the sweets section, Strate's cinnamon rolls and gourmet cupcakes from new vendor Sweet Josephine's of the Wilmington area did a fast vanishing act.

Also fast onto plates were lobster rolls, lobster macaroni-&-cheese and lobster tacos from New England Lobster, which flies in lobster on a daily basis to meet fairgoers' hearty demand.

Box Office Manager Trish Dunlap said her favorite had to be the pork nachos, while First Vice President Ken Clark marveled over the phenomenon of deep-fried foods at the fair, offering a growing menu including even deep-fried cookies, candy bars and ice cream.

"I'm surprised how transforming the deep-frying is," Clark said after sampling such a taco. "Doesn't taste like any taco I've ever had and the deep frying really wakes up the pickles and makes them zing."

DiMondi – who admitted his own partiality to the lobster rolls – said it was fun to host the fair folks' food finale. But he encouraged everyone who attends the fair to stroll the grounds and discover their own favorites, old and new, adding that new vendors are welcomed every year.

"The food always is a big part of the fair," he said. "I think we've raised the bar of culinary choices and quality."

To which a few happy and well-fed staff members chorused, "Amen."

LEGENDARY LITTLE RICHARD

Little Richard is a legend at the Delaware State Fair.

Not the Little Richard that's a singer-songwriter from Georgia, but another Little Richard who started out in the food business not long after World War II then bought the company in 1950.

And having had food booths at every Delaware State Fair starting in 1952, Richard Thomas has the honor of being the fair's longest-running vendor.

At first, he came down from Pennsylvania, but says he liked the fair and folks so much, he moved his family and business to Delaware.

Thomas has made his gratitude well-known with symbolic generosity, having given the fair two of its icons – a steer near the farm machinery and a carousel horse that graces the Administration Building, a gift in 2002 for his own 50th fair anniversary.

He retired in recent years back to Pennsylvania, but his business remains a fair

mainstay. And customers still see his face smiling from a 1952 photo on the popular Little Richard's refillable commemorative souvenir beverage cups.

His son-in-law, Dave Higman of Florida, now steers the operation of eight – yes, eight – Little Richard food stands that open each year at the fair, staffed by family and friends, including his wife Sandra, and two daughters.

Higman, who started coming to the fair in 1976, said Italian sausage, Philadelphia-style cheesesteaks, smoked turkey legs and Krispy Kreme doughnut burgers – with two full-sized, grilled donuts instead of the top and bottom of rolls – are the most popular food items among Delaware fairgoers.

Smoked turkey legs are even more popular farther south, he said, but he was touched when one fair customer told him that one of them meant a lot to her and her "Daddy."

Years ago, she told him, her father had terminal cancer and couldn't eat. One day, he told her he could eat a turkey leg from Little Richard's. So she drove to the fair and back, taking all day, but she never will forget seeing her father's face when she got home and watching him eat the whole leg, smiling the whole time.

"That was so nice to hear," he said, taking a brief break to chat at one of the tables by his family's biggest location, Little Richard's Café.

Such breaks – like a cool summer breeze – are rare at the fair for him and his crew. They start set up and deep clean each of their set-ups four full days before the fair opens and have thorough official inspections by the state Division of Public Health. There isn't a down moment until after the fair ends, Higman said, and even then, the crews do another deep cleaning on every set-up before they start packing.

With Little Richard's having been at the fair more than half its century, Higman said, he can't imagine what it was like 50 years before that. Or what it might be like in another 50 or 100 years.

For his father-in-law, the Delaware State Fair has created a lifetime of service and memories for himself, his wife Dolly, their children and their children's children.

He still remembers the old days when he sold French fries for 15 cents and ice cream for a dime as he traveled to fairs all over the country.

But he said the Delaware State Fair is the one he holds most dear.

"The fair's been very good to my family and I'm glad to be part of it," he said.

"It's my top fair in the country.... It always was."

FUN & GAMES

RENE VELASQUEZ OF Bridgeville barely could carry his massive prize from the midway, a plush unicorn almost as tall as he is.

"It's so big," said his 8-year-old daughter Sherlyn, who joined her father and 5-year-old brother John for a day of fun at the fair.

The big prize came from Velasquez's skill – and good luck – at one of the fair's oldest games, he said.

"You take the rings off the bottles and don't knock them down," he said.

"It's like fishing."

THRILL MACHINES

For L.J. and Elle Ford of Wilmington, going to the state fair is all about one thing.

"The rides!" they said in unison.

From there, however, their opinions differ.

Six-year-old Elle likes the Ferris wheel best, but big brother L.J., three years her senior, is all about the Mega-Drop.

Their father Russell Ford, who works in computer software, said the kids are still exploring and, someday, may like other rides better or something else altogether different about the fair.

"This is only our second year," he said.

His wife, stay-at-home mom Vicky Ford, said she's grateful to be able to have such a summertime family outing.

"I just like that our state has a state fair," she said.

BRINGING THE FUN

Rides and games have been a staple from the fair's earliest days.

In those days, rides were called mechanical amusements and some of the games later would be eliminated as thinly veiled gambling.

The fair's original directors hired the Krause Greater Show Company, then operating from Maine to Florida. Managed by Bennie Krause, that company was replaced in 1923 by the Greater West Shows' midway as an assortment of vaudeville performances grew along with the fair.

In 1928, Bruce's Greatest Shows was hired to present the midway, followed in 1931 by the West World Wonder Shows, then in 1935, Cetlin & Wilson Shows began a years-long run with the midway.

After the fair's World War II hiatus, there was a succession of midway companies – including one provider let go after its check to the fair bounced in the late 1940s.

Then Prell's Broadway Shows was hired for the midway, followed in the 1950s by Lawrence Greater Shows and returning for its last contract in 1960. Cetlin & Wilson got another midway contract, extending its run through 1969.

The following year started a new era, when the Delaware State Fair added the James E. Strates Shows as its amusement ride and carnival game provider in a relationship that would endure for decades.

The Strates Shows created a stir, arriving in Harrington as the last attraction of its kind to travel by train, drawing crowds to watch its crews unload. The Strates family became well-known figures here.

They bought land just behind the fairgrounds, spent time in Rehoboth Beach before the fair opened each year and always had their equipment serviced in Harrington during the fair.

"Now, we're almost relatives," E. James Strates once wrote to fair officials from his home in Florida.

One of the top amusements he brought to the fair was the only double-decker carousel in the United States.

But as years passed, the fair joined a growing number of state- and regional-level events shifting their midway amusement contracts to Wade Shows of Michigan.

Founded in 1912, Wade Shows has expanded over the last three decades to become the country's largest family-owned provider of carnival amusements.

Fair organizers praise the Wade organization's safety and professionalism, as well as its efforts to keep introducing new attractions while returning with longtime fair favorites.

The fair also has worked with Wade Shows to provide fairgoers with a variety of specials each year – such as discount ride wristbands – that help families stretch their entertainment dollars.

Wade's website boasts of having served more state fairs than any carnival company in history, maintaining more than 100 rides.

In addition to Delaware, Wade Shows now brings its fun and games to state fairs in Alabama, Florida, Missouri, North Carolina and Oklahoma.

Above: Frank Zaitshik, owner of Wade Shows

BLUE RIBBON QUEST

O**H, THE ALLURE** of being the best, earning the blue ribbon or winning as Grand Champion!

From the start a century ago, the Delaware State Fair has been the state's prime spot for residents to show their accomplishments – growing the range of competitions with every passing year.

Horse racing, which was the fair's signature contest from its debut, continues, but now shares the scene with hundreds of others.

Each year, tens of thousands of entries pour in, registering for contests, special events or the uncounted categories of competition for which the fair has become famous. In 2018 alone, the fair's 3,089 exhibitors totaled more than 41,000 competitive entries.

Competitions can be as heavy as beef cattle or as light as whimsical hats, floral arrangements and children's creations from duct tape.

And contests, too, run the full gamut from tractor pulls to specialized cooking events focused on foods from chocolate to Spam.

Above: Declan Baylis

Each exhibition entry must be carefully checked in, judged, displayed and readied for its scheduled return. And every entrant registration must be carefully recorded and tracked, lest a competitor be left out.

Administration behind management of the fair's entries is immense.

But so is the resulting satisfaction for winners, whether they have spent decades at the fair or are newcomers from first-year 4-H Club members completing their initial projects to aspiring young farmers with their first crops in FFA competition.

The late Mary Jester, an avid fair entrant who worked a 225-acre family farm with her husband and had a second job as a hairdresser, racked up more than 200 ribbons over years of needlework entries.

She was so proud of her first- and second-place Delaware State Fair ribbons that she stitched more than 150 of them to a quilt surrounding her name – and won her yet another blue ribbon.

Over the years, she became so accomplished, that she was honored with the Needlework Department's 1982 Hanson Memorial Award and made a needlework judge, which disqualified her from continuing in competition.

In tribute to both her talents and the fair, her family donated the ribbon-decorated quilt to the Harrington Museum, which displays her handiwork proudly, along with a wide array of fair memorabilia.

There, she is known as "The Queen of Blue Ribbons."

The museum, however, is on a blue-ribbon quest of its own.

Its collection of blue ribbons is just one short of complete.

For 1926, the seventh year of the fair, the museum's collection has only a red, second-place ribbon.

So – as with generations of state fair competitors striving to be the best – its blue-ribbon quest continues.

FRIENDLY CHALLENGE

George C. Simpson had one last competition in mind – and a trick up his sleeve – for a fellow farmer before retiring from the Delaware State Fair.

Born and raised on his family's farm in Houston, Simpson was a prominent dairy farmer who joined the fair in 1940, chairing the Swine and Dairy Department, serving on the executive committee and as vice president before becoming fair manager in 1962. Also involved in horse racing, he served as general manager of the Harrington Raceway and president of the Delaware Farm Bureau, in addition to being a lifetime member of Houston Fire Company.

The last competition he managed at the fair was a cow milking contest – with just two contestants and he was one of them.

Simpson issued his mano a mano challenge to Bridgeville farmer Thurman G. Adams Jr. Like Simpson, Adams had taken his place in a family farm. Adams also ran his family's business, T.G. Adams & Sons Inc. farm and grain business in Bridgeville.

A champion of agriculture in the state, Adams was a longtime fair supporter,

Above: Gary Simpson, George Simpson behind him

97

holding no-dividend stock, serving as an unpaid director and member of the executive committee.

Adams also was a powerful Sussex County Democrat, who chaired the Agriculture and Executive committees and went on to be the longest-serving state senator in Delaware history before he passed away in 2009.

Simpson's proposal of a contest in 1984 was, at one level, a bet between two Delaware farm boys and, at another, the ultimate Delaware State Fair showdown. The challenge also was something of a political showdown, as Simpson was a powerhouse Republican.

"It was a friendly challenge," recalled F. Gary Simpson, his uncle's successor as general manager, serving 1985-1992. News of the milking contest created quite a buzz in the Delaware Legislature, where the younger Simpson later would go on to serve five terms as a Republican state senator, retiring as Senate minority leader.

He chuckled as he revealed how his late uncle, who died in 1985, rigged the milking contest:

"He gave Thurman a dry cow."

Perhaps needless to say, the cow his uncle milked produced plenty.

And the one Adams had left the milk bucket dry.

The contest became a thing of Delaware State Fair legend.

And so did the way Adams later put his own spin on the results.

Adams didn't lie about losing, but he was known simply to omit the fact that there were only two of them in the competition.

"Whenever he told the story of the milking contest," Gary Simpson said, "he would say that he came in second and my uncle came in next to last."

FOR LOVE OF SPAM

Fair organizers love contests that create a lot of buzz.

And few created more buzz than the Delaware State Fair Best Spam Recipe Competition.

The 1996 contest proved popular with the public and the media, earning nearly a full page of coverage in the Delaware State News, headlined "Spam fans converge on fair."

Amy Calvert Welsh of Harrington took home first place with her Spam Chowder recipe.

Runner up was Jean Idler of Bridgeville with her Spam Lite Broccoli Cheese Ring and Brenda Wooten won third place with her Spam Spring Rolls. That year, Spam celebrated its 59th anniversary.

Judging the entries for taste appeal, recipe originality and appearance were retired Lake Forest School District home economics teacher Sarah Webb; Janet Scheidt, retired food services supervisor from the Caesar Rodney School District; retired Cape

Henlopen School District home economics teacher Beulah Sockrider, and then-Senator Thurmond Adams. In addition to cash prizes and bragging rights, winners they picked got ribbons, award certificates, official Spam aprons and the 48-page recipe booklet, "Great Taste of Spam."

Amy Welsh's Spam Chowder

12-ounce can of Spam Lite chopped in cubes
10¾ ounce can of cream of mushroom soup
14¾ ounce can of creamed corn
Small onion, diced
6 medium potatoes, diced small
3 cups of milk
Cup of broccoli, cut up

Melt margarine and saute onion in soup pot. Add cream corn, cream of mushroom soup, potatoes and milk. Cook approximately 20 minutes. When potatoes are almost done, add Spam and broccoli. Continue cooking slowly until desired consistency.

The Spam Recipe Contest later was phased out at the Delaware State Fair, but organizers say it could return as a flashback feature for the fair's upcoming centennial.

The inexpensive lunch meat, introduced in 1937 and sold in more than 99 percent of U.S. grocery stores, has proven popular over the years, with the Hormel company producing a "lite" version and variety of other styles, continuing its national-level cooking contest and even establishing a museum for Spam at its headquarters in Minnesota.

Before Spam hit 60, more than 5 billion cans were sold – enough to circle the Earth more than a dozen times. But Delaware isn't the First State when it comes to Spam or even in the top five. Top sales per capita are in Hawaii, Alaska, Arkansas, Texas and Alabama.

ON TRACK

HORSE RACING INTRODUCED Robert A. Holloway to the fair, when he was just a little kid – the latest generation in one of the families that has been involved the longest.

"I first went to the fair in 1936," said Holloway, who chairs the board's Concessions Committee. "My father said, 'You can't go until you're 6 years old and you can count."

There was good reason for that. His family had the racing program concession and he was to become their youngest salesman.

First, though, he had a lot of lessons in counting and making change, never using any kind off counter or calculator. "I made a penny on every program I sold," he recalled.

And soon, his carpenter's nail-bag apron was jingling with change. "I sold 200 of them... Then I went and spent a dollar at the midway."

He would go on to have a pony that won two of its three races, and get a wide-ranging experience of work that goes into presenting the fair – from peeling onions to checking fair IDs and, even as a kid, ejecting a few prominent violators.

"I had a great time," he said with a smile. "And I still do."

103

RACING EVOLUTION

Considering that Harrington was the heart of horse racing in Delaware, it only made sense that races would be a popular feature at the local fair.

As the fair celebrates its first century, that also marks 100 years of hard-running horses heading to the winner's circle.

Horse races were the fair's first contests. Motorcycle and automobile racing soon were added to the fair and quickly became popular.

Auto daredevil shows – best-known for their daring jumps – started to become big attractions at state fairs across the country in the 1940s and had become staples by the late 1950s and early 1960s.

But stock car races and other, similar forms of "wheel events" tended to tear up the track, forcing massive work that had to be done the same day or overnight by crews that initially were composed of fair directors, their families and friends. That was a lot to ask, but they did it to ready the track for the fair's following activities.

However, changing times that included some tragedies elsewhere led to the difficult decision that auto racing at the fair simply had to end.

Although no one wanted tragedies here, ultimately the precautions proved too prohibitive.

Modern safety standards, including specifications for barriers and crowd distance from the racers, would have required rebuilding the track or creating one just for motor sports. On top of that, although the state fair had a strong safety record with

few mishaps, the cost of insurance for race events steadily climbed in early years and skyrocketed over decades.

But the spirit stays alive with the annual Delaware State Fair Demolition Derby and a night of monster truck madness.

MOTOR MEMORIES

When he was just 5 years old, little Phil Davis of Delmar, Maryland, would go to the Kent and Sussex County Fair to see his father race his car.

Davis moved with his family to Delmar, Delaware, as a teen, enlisted in the service through Georgetown and later had a long career in building. Now, retired and living in Cambridge, Maryland, he has a part-time job delivering parts.

His childhood memories of his father racing may be a lifetime ago, but he said, "I could remember those memories like it was yesterday."

Although he never got into racing himself, those were the memories that got him hooked on the history of racing.

His collection of historic stock car photos in the region along with news articles, posters and other memorabilia – collected from anywhere he can find those treasures

– ultimately have become his main hobby and extensive enough to be featured in state-level displays.

"I'm still researching," he said. "I go to shows, but I don't sell. I mostly display my collection and do research." That includes looking to fill in blanks of racing results at the fair of his childhood, now the Delaware State Fair.

"They started the 'big car' races in Harrington in the 1920s," he said, adding that they moved to the Harrington fairgrounds from Elsmere, where an earlier fair went out of business.

"They were open wheel cars, like at Indianapolis, verses a stock car, and they called them 'big cars' because 'midget cars' existed elsewhere," he explained. Decades before its name changed to the Delaware State Fair, the Harrington track went big into stock cars.

"The stock cars first appeared at the Harrington fair in 1947," he said. "They lined up in front of the grandstands."

"The American Stock Car Racing Association out of Trenton [New Jersey] ran the first ones," Davis recalled. Then there was another national association, followed by the American Automobile Association, which evolved away from racing to the vehicle safety and emergency assistance organization it is today. Then, Davis said, there was the National Association for Stock Car Auto Racing.

"NASCAR did sanction some of the later races at the fair," he said.

But short of going to see the races, Davis said it was hard to find out who won. "There was a man who promoted races all over the country to tell you who would be there, but they never publicized the results. I would check all the old papers, the Delaware State News, the Harrington paper, the Milford Chronicle, sometimes The Sussex Countian, even though the races weren't in Sussex County, they sometimes had results."

For the open or big car racing, the United Racing Club was the final sanctioning organization, he said. "That's who was organizing the races when they had open-wheel ones at the end," he said. "Then they quit, I think 1955 was the last year."

Too many of those races ended in serious crashes, injuries and fatalities, he said.

The fair kept stock car racing, finally quitting those in 1998, he added.

Aside from issues of safety and insurance, Davis said, "the surface just wasn't conducive to car racing because it was a horse track. The way the cars are, with so much power, they would tear up the track and they were tearing down fences too."

Davis has watched other battles of motors and might – tractor pulls, the demolition derby and the like – but he says, "that's not my thing." Meanwhile, he is content to continue researching, collecting and learning more, especially about auto racing at the Delaware State Fair.

Davis is realistic about knowing that auto racing has become part of the fair's history, but he said, "I think people do miss it."

GROWLING ENGINES

For James W. Messick, devotion to the Delaware State Fair is a family affair.

"I inherited it from my father," said Messick – known to all as Jimmy – while the clock ticked toward the fair's popular monster truck and demolition derby events.

As chairman of the fair's motor sports or wheel events, Messick has to plan and supervise countless details of preparations, conscientiously sweating every detail to ensure both the safety and enjoyment of all who attend.

His is a huge commitment that takes plenty of time and lots of help, he said while pausing briefly from his tasks, "but there's no place I'd rather be."

Above: Jimmy Messick

Generations of the Messick family have been involved deeply in the fair, from exhibits to the prominent presence of longtime sponsor Taylor & Messick that typically dominates the farm machinery area.

Messick along with fellow director Jack Hendricks make the transformation happen as if on cue. It's not just a matter of setting up the track area for a demo derby or monster truck show, because they also have to tear down all that set-up and arrange – fast and in a very orderly fashion – the nearly 4,000 track chairs for the next concert.

At the 99th fair, Messick was deep into the home stretch of his motor sport preparations but made sure he found time to check in on how event ticket sales were going.

"A hundred tickets to go," he said with a smile after getting a report.

About 10 minutes later, "just 50 left."

Messick shifted his attention to some track details, personnel deployment and quick chat with fair officials before he got another ticket report.

"Sold out!" he said with a smile. "That's what we like to hear."

PASSING MENTION

Delaware State Fair has created countless happy memories for millions of guests over the years.

So when "The American State Fair" by Derek Nelson was released in 1999 by MBI Publishing Company, it made sense for Delawareans to check what the book has to say about our fair.

Sadly, though, the Delaware State Fair appears only as an illustration – the cover of the 45th annual Delaware State Fair Premium Book from 1964, with its promotions for the Joie Chitwood Thrill Show and other acts including singing sensation Bobby Vinton.

Although Chitwood's daredevil automobile show thrilled many a Delaware State Fair crowd, the cover merely illustrated the story of how he came to own the show.

Chitwood was on the crew of Earl "Lucky" Teter and his Hell Drivers, when Teter was killed in a crash during a 1942 benefit show for the Army Emergency Relief Fund.

Chitwood tried to handle the show's sale as a favor to the widow. But finding no takers, he borrowed money to buy it himself, going on to entertain crowds for decades in Delaware and across the country.

THAT'S ENTERTAINMENT

SOME FOLKS DON'T think twice about driving for hours – or booking a hotel – to catch a show at the Delaware State Fair.

That's the star power of the fair's headliners.

Marie Galasso and Dottie Bruntrager drove from New Hyde Park, New York, and got hotel rooms in Dover so they could catch the fair's Toby Keith concert.

"It took us more than five hours but there was traffic," Galasso said.

The drive definitely was worth it, they said, although they've been to other fairs that weren't.

They knew what to expect with their favorite star, but they weren't sure what to expect of the fair itself.

They arrived in plenty of time to check out the fair, wander through the dozens of food options and enjoy a good sausage-and-pepper sandwich before the show.

Although the friends said Toby Keith always is great,

On facing page:: Performer Hilby the German Juggle Boy and passenger
Top: Red Head Express
Center: Ridgeway & Johnson

111

they said they can't say the same thing about some of the other state fairs and venues where they went to catch his concerts.

But they said the Delaware State Fair scores an A+.

"I think the fair is very impressive," Galasso said. "It's so well organized and laid out, and it was very easy to find." And folks here are a lot more friendly than some of the fair crowds they've found elsewhere.

"We ran into a wounded vet and had a chance to talk to him and thank him," she said. "We bought him lunch and thanked him for fighting for us every step of the way.… "

"We're having a great time," Bruntrager said.

And both said the concert was a bargain for the time and expense of attending.

Awaiting another show, a group of Sussex County residents – and a trio of Delaware natives who had moved to Maryland and Pennsylvania – harmonized their own version of the often-recorded "Let the Good Times Roll."

Although they didn't want to share their names, with one saying his name is "Anonymous" and another joking that he's in the U.S. Federal Witness Protection Program, they said the growth of headliners' evening concerts has been the best thing that could happen to the fair.

The fair regulars said they meet at the fair, spend the day exploring exhibits, catching some rides and buying an eclectic array of food for dinner, then go enjoy the concert.

"You see people here that you can't see anywhere else in Delaware," one woman said.

As with many concerts or tours that are underwritten to varying degrees by supporters, sponsorships help make booking, promoting and hosting such headliners possible. The Summer Concert Series is presented by the Delaware Lottery at the grandstands sponsored by M&T Bank.

The 2018 fair saw the debut of another stage at the new Hertrich Plaza in front of the Grandstands, where free concerts by Red Head Express and Vocal Trash drew crowds daily, often more than filling the casual seating with listeners standing nearby.

That venue, like others, serves double-duty between performances for both fun and education – as the setting of the Sussex County Health coalition's Healthy Kids Fair and a one-day "chicken-pick'n" contest sponsored by Mountaire to see who could pick and shred the most meat from a cooked chicken.

Offering different sizes of stages and other entertainment spots is a longtime strength of the fair because it has given many local or regional groups exposure they wouldn't get in a typical nightclub gig, said fair regular Dennis Cresswell.

"I saw the MarDels there I don't know how many times," he said. "They're great."

So is the state fair overall, he said, adding that even though it's a bit of a drive from New Castle County, "I wouldn't miss it."

His loyalty was well-rewarded at the 2018 fair.

Cresswell won a pair of tickets to the sold-out Toby Keith concert.

"Great concert," he later posted on Facebook, as friends congratulated him on his luck.

Even getting the tickets in a giveaway by 94.7 WDSD "Delaware's Country Station" was a major experience, he said.

"So excited, Whiskey and Randy presented the

At right: Prize winner Dennis Cresswell, center, with WDSD personalities tickets to me," he said, adding, "WDSD 94.7. The best in country music…. I should do a commercial."

Lucky winners got tickets from WDSD and other radio stations broadcasting live from the fair not only the Toby Keith, Brett Eldredge, Chris Young and Southern Uprising concerts but also the Monster Truck Meltdown, performance by ventriloquist Jeff Dunham and the fair's now-annual Craft Beer Festival.

That festival is one of the fair's newest traditions.

Tying into the international renaissance of craft brewing offered an opportunity to create a new event with entertainment options suited to folks who like to relax and drink a beer or two while enjoying their music. And concert-goers agreed.

"This is such a great idea," Pat Sparks of Milford said as she moved forward in the long – but chatty-friendly and quickly moving – line for the event's debut in 2017. She called organizers' choice of pairing craft beer and classic rock-and-roll "a perfect match... two of my favorite things."

"I've always loved the state fair and I'm glad to see that they will start something new like this but keep so much of what's traditional," she said, adding that the combination keeps her coming back.

Young entertainers such as the Lake Forest High School Marching Band and Color Guard also keep coming back to entertain fair guests at other spots on the grounds, such as the area of the Mann-Tharp Pavilion.

"This is my fourth year," said 17-year-old trombonist Alora Baker, a senior who lives just outside Harrington and had another role at the fair, working at the poultry barn.

The enthusiastic band, directed by Christopher Patterson, practiced eight songs and coordinated with the quick-stepping color guard dancers for their annual fair performances that included the fair's Spirit of America Military Day.

The teens – and quite a few of their family members – beamed when their patriotic tunes and dance performance drew cheers and applause.

Packing the 10-day fair with entertainment takes year-round planning that starts pretty much as soon as the fair closes, General Manager Bill DiMondi said. "It's a lot of work," he said, "but it's definitely worth it."

CAVALCADE OF STARS

Starting in 1955, the Delaware State Fair modernized entertainment, shifting from musical revues and vaudeville shows to headline musicians, well-known celebrities, special shows and high-interest competitions.

Other popular entertainment continues to include the fair's annual demolition derby, monster truck night and traditional harness racing on Governor's Day. Through the years, fair entertainment also has featured a variety of stock car races, auto stunt shows and kart competitions.

On some occasions, Delaware State Fair concert-goers get to see multiple headliners in one show, thanks to the trend of entertainers planning tours together with a favorite warm-up act or other groups expected to share their audiences. For example, "An Evening of Doo Wop," starred Little Anthony & the Imperials, along with The Drifters, The DuPrees, The Flamingos and The Chiffons.

Bottom: Danny Aguilar, Variety Attractions owner George Moffett, Chubby Checker, Todd Boltin, the fair's talent buyer from Variety Attractions

Here is the "Who's Who" – and when's when – of Delaware State Fair's top entertainment.

A

A Great Big World – 2016
Roy Acuff & The Smokey Mountain Boys – 1961
Bryan Adams – 2015
Trace Adkins – 2008, 2013
Clay Aiken – 2004
Air Supply – 1981
Alabama – 1992, 1993, 1998, 2016
Jason Aldean – 2010, 2012
All-Star Professional Wrestling – 1986, 1987
All Star Weekend – 2010
All-Youth Talent Contest – 1985, 1988
All-Youth Talent Showcase – 1995
Deborah Allen – 1993
Jimmie Allen – 2018
America – 2004
Bill Anderson – 1977
Lynn Anderson – 1968, 1973
Antique Tractor Pull – 1997, 1998
Eddie Arnold – 1969
The Ataris – 2006
Rodney Atkins – 2008, 2010
Frankie Avalon – 1959

B

The Band Perry – 2011
The Banana Splits – 1970
Moe Bandy – 1985
Ava Barber – 1976
Batman & Robin – 1975
The Beach Boys – 1969, 2006, 2010
Dierks Bently – 2009, 2013
Big Daddy Weave – 2017
Big & Rich – 2006
Big Time Rush – 2011
The Bitter End Singers – 1965
Clint Black – 1995
Blood, Sweat & Tears – 1977
Blues Traveler – 2016
Pat Boone – 1956

Ash Bowers – 2010
Bob Boylan – 1965
Boxcar Willie – 1984
Craig Wayne Boyd – 2015
Boyz II Men – 1995
Brass Construction – 1978
Bread – 1971
Brooks & Dunn – 1995, 1996, 2000, 2002, 2008
Bruce in the USA – 2018
Luke Bryan – 2013
Building 429 – 2012
Bob Burgess – 1965

C

Chris Cagle – 2002
Jeremy Camp – 2014
Craig Campbell – 2011
Glen Campbell – 1982
Jo Ann Campbell & the Twist-O-Rama – 1962
Carman – 1993
Jason Michael Carroll – 2007
Carrot Top – 2003
The Carter Family – 1981
Tommy Cash – 1970

Above: Meghan Trainor

Casting Crowns – 2012, 2015
Jo Ann Castle – 1961
Champagne Champagne – 2011
Greyson Chance – 2011
Steven Curtis Chapman – 1991
Cheap Trick – 2012
Kenny Chesney – 2004
Chic – 1979
Chicago Knockers – 1983
The Chiffons – 2007
The Chordettes – 1959
Eric Church – 2006, 2011
Circus Continental – 1989
Circus Kingdom – 1993
Cirque Odyssey – 2005
Roy Clark – 1973
Kelly Clarkson – 2009
Jerry Clower – 1997
Reno Collier – 2012
Color Me Badd – 1992
Luke Combs – 2017
David Cook – 2009
Easton Corbin – 2010
Bill Cosby – 2002, 2007
Miranda Cosgrove – 2011
Country Comfort – 1997
Country Music Talent Contest
– 1977, 1978, 1979, 1980, 1981
Country Showdown competition
– 1984, 1985, 1986, 1987
The Cover Girls – 1991
Bucky Covington – 2008
Cowboy Troy – 2006
The Cowsills – 1968

Floyd Cramer – 1975
Crowder – 2017
Clay Culhane – 1960

D

Lauren Daigle – 2018
Charlie Daniels Band – 1984, 1987, 2005, 2018
Daughtry – 2007, 2008
Danny Davis & the Nashville Brass – 1976
Skeeter Davis – 1975
Dennis Day – 1967
Jimmy Dean – 1958
Paula Deen – 2010
Delaware Cheerleading Championship
– 1988, 1996
Def Leppard – 2000
Gavin DeGraw – 2005
Delaware Volunteer Firefighters' Pro Rodeo
– 2014, 2015
Delmarva Sunday Spectacular with Hoppy
Adams – 1979
Joe Diffie – 1996
Dion – 1961
The Tommy Dorsey Orchestra – 1983
The Doodletown Pipers – 1971
Mike Douglas – 1966
The Drifters – 2007
Roy Drusky – 1978
Arthur Duncan – 1977
Jeff Dunham – 2009, 2013, 2016, 2018
The Duprees – 2007

E

Eagles Experience – 2018
The Edwardians – 1976
Brett Eldredge – 2014, 2018
Gloria Estefan & the Miami Sound Machine
– 1988
Exile – 1986

F

The Fabulous Thunderbirds – 2016
Barbara Fairchild – 1974
Rachel Farley – 2012
Joe Feeney – 1979
Jordan Feliz – 2016

Above: The Cowsills

Freddy Fender – 1976
Ferko String Band – 1985
Finger Eleven – 2013
Firefighter Combat Challenge – 1997
First State Force – 1990
The Flamingos – 2007
Rascal Flatts – 2004, 2005, 2017
Flo Rida – 2009
Myron Floren – 1961, 1972
Florida Georgia Line – 2013
Sally Flynn – 1975
Flynnville Train – 2007
Red Foley – 1959, 1962
Frank Fontaine – 1963, 1967
For King & Country – 2015, 2016
Colt Ford – 2012
The Four Lads – 1957
The Four Seasons – 1963, 1967, 1975
The Four Tops – 1991
Peter Frampton – 2006
David Frizzell – 1984

G

Gaelforce Dance – 1999
Gary & Tomio – 1983
Larry Gatlin & the Gatlin Brothers – 1980
Crystal Gayle – 1979
Brantley Gilbert – 2014, 2017
Vince Gill – 1992, 1997
The Gin Blossoms – 2009
Arthur Godfrey & Goldie – 1964
The Happy Goodman Singers – 1974
Grand Funk Railroad – 2015
Amy Grant – 1995
Lee Greenwood – 2002

Guy & Ralna – 1971, 1973

H

Merle Haggard & the Strangers – 1971
The Hamid-Morton Circus – 1975
Clay Hart – 1975
Tony Hawk's Boom Boom Huck Jam – 2008
Barbara Heller – 1964
The Henningsens – 2013
Hinder – 2008
The Hinsons – 1984
Al Hirt – 1969
Hodges – 2008
Will Hoge – 2013
Hoobastank – 2005
Larry Hooper – 1965
Hot Chelle Rae – 2011
Julianne Hough – 2009
Howdy Doody with Buffalo Bob – 1973
The Hubcaps – 1984
Huckleberry Hound – 1961
Eric Hutchinson – 2009

I

Gabriel Iglesias – 2017
iMPACT Wrestling presented by TNA – 2011
Jack Ingram – 2007
International All-Girl Mud Wrestling – 1984
The Irish Rovers – 1969

J

Alan Jackson – 1991, 1993, 1997, 2011
Stonewall Jackson – 1975
Jade – 1993
Sonny James – 1970
Jet Black Stare – 2008

Top: Sugarland
Bottom: Little Big Town

Jethro Tull – 2000
Joan Jett & the Blackhearts – 1987
Kamey Johnson – 2010
George Jones – 1985, 1995
The Judds – 1989
Victoria Justice – 2013

K

Kalin & Myles – 2013
KC & the Sunshine Band – 1976, 1999
Toby Keith – 2003, 2004, 2005, 2007, 2011, 2018
Emmett Kelly Jr. with circus acts – 1974
Ke$ha – 2011
Kool & the Gang – 1980

L

The LACS – 2014
Lady Antebellum – 2007, 2008, 2014
Miranda Lambert – 2012
Chris Lane – 2017
Larry the Cable Guy – 2003, 2005, 2006, 2012
Tracy Lawrence – 1996
Le Roux – 1982
Brenda Lee – 1963, 1966
The Lennon Sisters – 1962
Gary Lewis & the Playboys – 1966
Jerry Lee Lewis – 1972
Little Anthony & the Imperials – 2007
Little Big Town – 2016
Live – 2003
Alice Lon – 1960
The Lone Ranger & Tonto
– 1957, 1960, 1965

Lonestar – 2000
Demi Lovato – 2009
Patty Loveless – 1992
Lower Case Blues – 2015, 2016
Sandy Luce & her All-Girl Thrill Show
– 1963, 1965
Dustin Lynch – 2015
Loretta Lynn – 1971, 1981, 1998
Lynyrd Skynyrd – 1998, 1999, 2005, 2010

M

Austin Mahone – 2013
Marshall Tucker Band – 1997, 2018
Barbara Mandrell – 1990
Louise Mandrell – 1985
The Mariners – 1955
Kathy Mattea – 1989
Martina McBride – 2000, 2008
McClain – 2014
Charly McClain – 1983
Neal McCoy – 1998
Ronnie McDowell – 1988
Reba McEntire – 1988, 1999, 2000
Tim McGraw – 1998
Brian McKnight – 2000
MercyMe – 2013
Jo Dee Messina – 2001
Midland – 2017
The Midwestern Hayride – 1956
The Glenn Miller Orchestra – 1982
Milli Vanilli – 1990
Ronnie Milsap – 1985
Mr. Mister – 1986

Left: Luke Bryan
Right: Toby Keith

Justin Moore – 2012
Craig Morgan – 2010
Lorrie Morgan – 1995
Moto-X Championships – 2002

N

Willie Nelson & Family – 1987, 1988, 2002
Tom Netherton – 1980
Natalie Nevins – 1966
The New Christy Minstrels – 1967
New Found Glory – 2010
New Kids on the Block – 1989, 2015
Joe Nichols – 2014
Nickelodeon's U Pick Nick – 1997
Britt Nicole – 2014

O

The Oak Ridge Boys – 1980, 1989
Tony Orlando & Dawn – 1974
K.T. Oslin – 1990
The Outlaws – 2018
O-Town – 2001
Jake Owen – 2016
Bonnie Owens – 1971
Buck Owens – 1972

P

Painted Pony Rodeo – 2017
Brad Paisley – 2002, 2006, 2007, 2009, 2010
Paramore – 2010
Jon Pardi – 2017
Twila Paris – 1991
Drew Parker – 2018
Dolly Parton – 1969
Sandi Patti – 1992, 2002
Les Paul & Mary Ford – 1960, 1963
Minnie Pearl – 1961
Pentatonix – 2013
Kelly Pickler – 2007
The Pistol Annies – 2012
Rachel Platten – 2016
Plus One – 2001
Popeye, the Sailor Man – 1958
Charley Pride – 1970, 1979, 1982, 1991
Jordan Pruitt – 2009

Q

Carmel Quinn & the Nashvillians
– 1961, 1962

R

Boots Randolph – 1975
Rare Earth – 1972
The Rascals – 1967
Susan Raye – 1972
Re-Creation – 1986, 1987
REO Speedwagon – 2005
The Righteous Brothers – 1965
Jeannie C. Riley – 1965
Tex Ritter – 1961
Road USA – 1997
Jimmy Roberts – 1966
Rock of the '70s – 2017
Johnny Rodriguez – 1974
Kenny Rogers – 1993, 2000
Kenny Rogers & the First Edition – 1973
Royal Danish Circus – 1977
Royal Palace Circus – 1978
Darius Rucker – 2009, 2017
Bobby Rydell – 1983

Top: Jimmie Allen
Bottom: Florida Georgia Line

S

Sandi & Shelly – 1970
Savage Garden – 1998
Sawyer Brown – 1999
Dylan Scott – 2018
Seduction – 1990
Serendipity Singers – 1964, 1968
Shai – 1993
Shenendoah – 1991
Blake Shelton – 2002
Jean Shepard – 1978
The Shirelles – 1983
Sidewalk Prophets – 2016
Ricky Skaggs – 1983
Canaan Smith – 2012
Connie Smith – 1970
Granger Smith – 2016
Michael W. Smith – 1996
The Speer Family – 1984
The Spin Doctors – 1995
Spirit of the Dance – 2003, 2004
Staind – 2004, 2008
Sally Starr – 1964, 1968
The Statler Brothers – 1974
Steel Magnolia – 2010

Stevie B – 1991
Doug Stone – 1990
George Strait – 1992
Striking Matches – 2014
Styx – 2005, 2012
Sugarland – 2007. 2012
Super Kid Variety Show, cartoon characters – 1978
Taylor Swift – 2007
The Sylvers – 1997

T

Tegan & Sara – 2010
The Temptations – 1991
38 Special – 2006
BJ Thomas – 1970
George Thorogood & The Destroyers – 2016
Three Days Grace – 2011
Three Dog Night – 2004
3 Doors Down – 2008, 2013
Tiffany – 1989
Pam Tillis – 1996
Mel Tillis – 1981
Nick Todd – 1958
T-Pain – 2009
Train – 2014
Meghan Trainor – 2015
Jim Travis – 1996
Randy Travis – 1990, 2001
The Trews – 2011
Travis Tritt – 2003, 2018
Ginny Tui – 1965
Josh Turner – 2011, 2015

Top: 3 Doors Down
Middle: George Thorogood
Bottom: Rascal Flatts

Mary Lou Turner – 1977
TV Cartoon Characters – 1972
12 Stones – 2007
Conway Twitty – 1960, 1983, 1986

U
Uncle Kracker – 2004
Carrie Underwood – 2007, 2008
Keith Urban – 2003, 2014
V
Ricky Van Shelton – 1990
Variety Show with Little El, magician,
animal performers – 1976
Velasquez – 2001
The Village People – 1999
Bobby Vinton – 1964
W
Porter Wagoner – 1969
Morgan Wallen – 2017
Wallenda Duo – 1993
Warner Brothers Cartoon Characters
– 1971
Gene Watson – 1987
Jimmy Wayne – 2009
Weinerville – 1998
Kitty Wells – 1961
Shelly West – 1984

Chuck Wicks – 2009
Wild Cherry – 1978
Hank Williams Jr. – 1968
Zach Williams – 2018
Gretchen Wilson – 2006
Windley the Wizard – 1980
Lee Ann Womack – 2002
Wrestling – 2001
Tammy Wynette – 1995
X, Y & Z
X Ambassadors – 2016
Yellow Card – 2006
Dwight Yoakam – 2001
Yogi Bear – 1961
Chris Young – 2008, 2010, 2018
Stars of "The Young & The Restless" – 1990
Young MC – 1990
Young Steff – 2009
Your Father's Mustache – 1968

Left: Jason Aldean
Right: Alan Jackson

DEBUT OF HEADLINERS

From the start of the 100-year-old Delaware State Fair – first known as the Kent and Sussex County Fair – providing entertainment for the region's residents has been a top priority.

Early on, live entertainment at the Harrington fairgrounds was dominated by musical revues featuring costumed women dancing.

But that changed in 1955 when the fair board – led by President Jacob O. Williams – made a bold and successful move.

That's when the fair hired its first headline act, known across the country and beyond.

The Mariners were a four-man gospel and pop singing group, started in New York City in 1942.

They toured New England states and performed at U.S. military bases in the Pacific in 1945.

Broadcasts of some of those shows landed them a recurring spot on celebrity Arthur Godfrey's radio show, which led to television appearances.

They made their debut as recording artists in 1949 on the Columbia Records label.

Their first big hit was "They Call the Wind Maria," an often-recorded song by Alan J. Lerner with lyrics by Frederick Loewe for their 1951 Broadway hit musical, "Paint Your Wagon."

Within two years came their biggest hit, "I See the Moon" – another popular song that would see many recordings and is said to have been derived from a simple couplet of British poetry dating from the 1700s:

I see the moon and the moon sees me

God bless the moon and God bless me

The song and the fame it brought proved a blessing for the uncommon, interracial musical group that performed it as well at the Delaware State Fair, then known as the Kent and Sussex County Fair.

That year's fair included Delaware Governor J. Caleb Boggs leading the dedication of a new fairgrounds grandstands that cost $350,000 – equivalent to more than $3 million in today's dollars – and the fair booking The Mariners to help fill its seats.

A news article of the day described the grandstands as "modern in every detail," adding that it "won the enthusiastic approval of fair patrons."

So did The Mariners.

Although "the well known radio and TV quartet got slightly more than damp as they went through their act despite the showers," one news account of the day said, the rain "failed to dampen the enthusiasm of the closing night crowd."

And from then on, its officials said, the fair always has tried to book crowd-pleasing headliners.

Although The Mariners' fame would fade in the years after their groundbreaking appearance at the Harrington fairgrounds, a recording has been made of their compiled songs and some 45s may be found for sale online.

And in a special tribute, one of their records permanently hangs framed in the Delaware State Fair Administration Building, in honor of their historic impact on entertainment at the event.

Left: Brad Paisley
Right: Lady Antebellum

STAGE NOTES

In 1991, Charley Pride set a record for the most shows by a single performer, having already appeared in 1970, 1979 and 1982.

Half a dozen more popular acts would go on to share his four-year status.

They include Alabama, the Charlie Daniels Band, Alan Jackson and Lynyrd Skynyrd on the musical side, along with a pair of entertainers – comedian Larry the Cable Guy and ventriloquist Jeff Dunham.

In 2008, Brooks & Dunn set a new record with five years of performances, matched two years later by Brad Paisley. And a pair of country music showcases, each running five years, set the performance contest record.

But a new entertainment record was set in the 99th year of the fair, with the return of Toby Keith.

He already had matched Brad Paisley and Brooks & Dunn at five years of entertaining crowds at the fair with such success, that his 2018 appearance – marking his sixth – made him the lone and undisputed record holder.

Not all acts, however, have gone so well.

Left: Carrie Underwood
Right: Charlie Daniels

In a sadder cancellation, Eddie Rabbitt was scheduled to perform in 1985 but dropped out after his son died several weeks before the fair. George Jones was booked to take his place in the concert lineup.

Skeeter Davis and Stonewall Jackson performed July 19, 1975, even though Lefty Frizzell, who was supposed to be their co-headliner, died that morning of a massive stroke.

Crystal Gayle bowed out of her scheduled 1978 appearance due to illness. Her performance was replaced with a free show by the winner of that year's Country Music Talent Contest, Dave Speicher & the Astrotones.

Disney pop star Selena Gomez also canceled a sold-out show, disappointing 9,600 young ticket-holding fans just days before her scheduled performance in 2010.

And a 2015 cancellation turned the night to wreckage, literally. When Little Big Town couldn't make it that Friday night, the fair hosted a Championship Demolition Derby.

Two shows that didn't cancel made fair history.

New Kids on the Block and co-headliner Tiffany set the box office record for attendance in 1989, each selling out two shows on the same night.

TV star Lawrence Welk never appeared at the Delaware State Fair, but many of his singers, musicians and dancers did.

Although modern-day music competition shows are producing a fair number of stars, The Lawrence Welk Show remains the top star-maker in terms of fair entertainment.

Best known among them were The Lennon Sisters, whose harmonies rocketed them to national stardom. Others were Lynn Anderson, Ava Barber, Bob Boylan, Bob Burgess, Jo Ann Castle, Arthur Duncan, The Edwardians, Joe Feeney, Myron Floren,

Above: Taylor Swift

Sally Flynn, Guy & Ralna, Clay Hart, Larry Hooper, Alice Lon, Natalie Nevins, Jimmy Roberts and Sandi & Sally.

In 1958, Jimmy Dean was the first big-name country music star to headline at the fair.

And while the fair typically offers all kinds of entertainment and a variety of types of music every year – often including rock and teen pop – the various kinds of country music together have remained the most popular.

Left: Travis Tritt
Right: Keith Urban

Top left: First State Force
Top right: Sally Starr

EXOTIC ANIMALS

THE CAMEL SHOW, petting zoo and exotic animals are a big hit at the fair – and the fact that they're free impresses a lot of parents with gaggles of kids in tow.

"It's a nice opportunity," said Michelle Biggs, a Greenwood homemaker visiting the fair with relatives and friends. "I'd have to say that the food and exotic animals are my favorite part of the fair."

The youngest of her companions said the petting zoo was their favorite part of the fair.

"I like the animals best," said family friend, 5-year-old Daniel Swartzenturber.

Four-year-old Daysi Biggs was even more specific about her favorite.

"Giraffes," she said with a giggle. "Giraffes, giraffes, giraffes."

Feeding animals carrot sticks made a big impression on 2-year-old Landon Trimball of Laurel, even if he did call the veggie pieces something that sounded like "Fresh fries."

135

The variety of such obviously healthy animals, the carrots and other wholesome snacks available for kids to feed them, large pens with spotless straw bedding, the fresh air and convenient hand sanitizer stations impressed Bonnie Smithson, 61, of Kent County, Maryland.

"It's just so nice and clean and wonderful, especially for the children," she said, adding that the farm equipment and animals are always her favorite parts of the fair.

"I just love it all," she said. "I don't know how anybody could not love the Delaware State Fair."

CHECK OUT THE SHOPPING

Tᴇɴ-ʏᴇᴀʀ-ᴏʟᴅ Iᴢᴀʙᴇʟ Wɪʟsᴏɴ of Georgetown says she still loves fair food, the demolition derby still is awesome and there are a lot of other great things to do.

But now she has a different favorite thing at the Delaware State Fair.

That's the shopping.

The first thing she wanted to do when she got to the fairgrounds with her mother, Sussex County Paramedic Heather Wilson, was "find the toe rings."

So they did.

Once Izabel picked out her favorite from a midway vendor's hundreds of toe rings, next up was shopping for school clothes – and her mother didn't mind a bit.

"Simply Southern is a brand of clothes that she really likes and they're hard to find," she said.

While back-to-school shopping at the state fair might seem to court the end of summer just a bit too much, early birds flocked to a booth packed with Christmas ornaments and others bought everything from lobster bisque to German knives to bamboo bed linens.

139

Telescoping flag poles may be purchased just a short walk from "The World's Best Hummingbird Feeder," water softening systems, hand-blended essential oils, custom tubs, outfits for babies and organic treats for pets. Not to mention plenty of Delaware State Fair clothing and souvenirs, gearing up for special offerings during the 2019 centennial run.

For some fairgoers, like Phil and Bev Marvel of Milton, one summer's browsing at the fair can lead to the next summer's shopping there.

Phil Marvel said the animals always are his favorite part of the fair, but he agreed when his wife said the most fun "is seeing the fair through the eyes of our grandchildren."

And they also agreed on a bit of shopping. "We saw the telescoping flag poles last year," the husband said, "and we came back to get one this year."

A few limited souvenirs started out as the fair's only merchandise beyond food, but the market has grown steadily in size and diversity.

Decades ago, fair officials decided to grow the shopping experience for fairgoers. They aimed to bring in options that might otherwise be too far away to find, while continuing to emphasize the local business community.

More and more frequently, newcomers are artisans, artists or experts in specialized crafts, including things such as custom signs and bracelets, made while their buyers watch.

Mamie Handy of Laurel, who attends the fair every year, said the crafts are her favorite part of the fair.

On a continuing basis, more than half the new vendors are Delaware-based.

With hundreds of businesses and agencies vying for fairgoers' attention and competing with online merchandising, many take advantage of the fair's high-volume foot traffic to introduce their products and services with demonstrations, samples, discounts and coupons – and, of course, freebies.

FAIREST OF THE FREEBIES

Goodies, giveaways, freebies or swag.

Sure, help yourself.

No matter what it's been called over the years, stuff that's free for the taking is a longtime tradition at the Delaware State Fair.

Jeffrey Gentry of Chesapeake City, Maryland, said he'll never forget going to the fair and collecting free pens, pencils, erasers, notebooks and wooden rulers – with perfect back-to-school timing from politicians, exhibitors and vendors.

"That's what I remember most about the fair as a kid," he said. "Coming to the fair to collect school supplies."

He remembers the process like shopping, but not having to pay for anything.

Flash forward to see Gentry all grown up and on the other side of the table.

Now working as a communications specialist in the state Department of Health and Social Services, he found himself in charge of the agency's fair booth.

And he certainly did not disappoint.

Of course, there was plenty of important information in brochures, cards, stickers and magnets about topics from help for addiction to reporting elder abuse.

Then there were the freebies: Stainless steel travel cups, fidget-spinners, thumb drives, hand sanitizer, sun screen, Band-Aids, several styles of tote bags, plastic mugs, lip balm and pens – and PopSockets, those collapsible circle gizmos that stick to the back of cellphones and other devices to make them easier to hold or stand up hands-free.

To promote the booth, DHSS Secretary Kara Odom Walker, Director of Communications Jill Fredel and department staff live-streamed daily "swag bag" giveaways to random winners from Facebook entries.

Gentry's lone disappointment: "The thing I miss is, we don't have wooden pencils and rulers. And I wish we did."

But other booths had pencils aplenty and the Fire School of Delaware had lots of wooden rulers, along with other goodies including Smarties with fire-safety messages.

Another standout for freebies: Food Lion Hunger Relief Day.

Many at the fair filled a variety freebie tote bags with cups, mugs, pens, pencils, crayons, easy-grip jar openers, recipe cards, flash lights, candy and snacks being given out at multiple spots.

Among other popular freebies: Heavy plastic ponchos and tire-pressure gauges from the Division of Motor Vehicles, safety flashers and kid-style hard hats from the Department of Transportation, Tic Tac-style mints from Delmarva Poultry Industry Inc., microfiber eyeglass cleaners from the Division for the Visually Impaired, tuna can drainers from De.Gov/BuyLocal, emery boards from the Delaware Criminal Justice Information System and fly-swatters from the Office of the State Insurance Commissioner.

But on hot days at the fair, the freebie that is thought to have been the first may be the most popular.

That's a good, old-fashioned fan.

Freebies and shopping at the fair are great, said Laura Baker of Bear. But her favorite souvenir of the fair always will be an old snapshot of her with her husband, John.

UNIQUE MARKETING OPPORTUNITY

The Delaware State Fair is good for business, says Arthur Carver IV, and it's a great way to help a tasty business grow.

What brings Carver back to the fair from North Carolina each year is the opportunity to meet a lot of people – and give free samples of a soda they might not see in their grocery stores – yet.

143

That's Cheerwine, a super-bubbly non-alcoholic cherry soda named a century ago for its perky nature and deep color.

With about 15,000 fairgoers taste-testing every year, Carver said, "It's a big hit."

Expanding the 101-year-old soda's region takes a supply chain, distributors and retailer cooperation, he said, but "you have to get people to try the product."

Existing distribution reaches as far north as Smyrna and Chestertown, Maryland, Carver said, but the added exposure at the fair could be key to growing Cheerwine's availability.

"We're a small family company with less than 20 employees," said Carver, regional sales manager for Carolina Beverage Corp., which began crafting the soda in 1917. So being at the Delaware State Fair represents a large and important investment for the company based 400 miles away in Salisbury, North Carolina.

Cheerwine has grown partnerships on the fairgrounds with the Delaware Farm Bureau, Grange and others who add the soda to their menus, as well as the fair administration. Cheerwine is now available in vending machines on the fairgrounds and, at the Loyal Order of Moose Chapter 1229 food booth, it's a popular beverage choice advertised by its distinctive bottlecap attached to the roof.

Booth volunteers even recommend the soda to go with the signature Moose snack. "How is Cheerwine?" one asks, repeating a customer's question. "Cheerwine is great. And it goes great with our Moose ears, which are $5 each or three for $12."

Bottom right: Laura and John Baker

CAMPING AT THE FAIR

Long ago, people who brought animals to the fair would snuggle up next to their cows or sheep at the end of a long day.

Or they might catch a few ZZZs in their truck.

Long ago, too, it was a common sight to see carnival workers trying to sleep on the rides or inside the train cars that brought them.

But now they have a choice. And hundreds of them opt for the choice of staying at the Delaware State Fair campgrounds.

In 1967, the fair established "camping in the grove," welcoming fairgoers with trailers, trucks, campers and tents.

Over the years, electricity and more space have been added to the increasingly popular facility.

147

More than 390 exhibitors, about 110 commercial vendors and a growing number of members of the public now make the campground their homes-away-from-home during the fair. Some stay just a night, while others camp here for the entire run of the fair.

"It's just so convenient," one dairy farmer said. "Better than sleeping next to your cow or not sleeping at all."

Row after row of recreational vehicles, trucks with pop-up tents and other camping variations create something of a sub-community here. Fees vary, but camper after camper says it's cheaper and more convenient than booking a hotel, but mainly a lot more friendly fun.

Someone wandering through might be invited by families of strangers to stop and sit for a cold beverage, hot meal or a friendly visit in this down-home version of tailgate living.

Here, they hang out flags and family signs, put tablecloths on their picnic tables and sometimes play a little music when they're in between things at the fair.

"I'd have to say that camping in the grove with friends and family is my favorite part of the fair," said longtime exhibitor Jean Thomas of Marydel. "I've been coming 46 years... since I was born."

Another camper less than half her age but also a longtime exhibitor, 19-year-old Jorda Shuba of Wyoming, said he couldn't wait to get checked in and settled.

"Camping at the fair is the best," he said.

ABOUT THE KIDS

U.S. SENATOR CHRIS Coons said, "My favorite part of the fair is seeing kids who are part of FFA and 4-H, who are just so excited about showing their animals and their exhibits."

"Those are both programs that so do much to help young Delawareans grown their confidence and skills," Coons said.

Of course, there are great entertainers and attractions, interesting business and agency exhibits, fun amusements, shows and rides, along with great fair food options, he said.

And there are plenty of constituents to visit with and share opinions with about all sorts of issues.

"But what I get the most out of these days," the senator said with a smile, "is seeing our young Delawareans."

That's a sentiment shared by Delaware Senator Ernie Lopez of Lewes, who works

with youngsters and their parents as a 4-H extension specialist through the University of Delaware.

Lopez, who made Delaware history in 2012 as the first Latino elected to the state Senate, says preparing for and entering the fair helps youngsters develop leadership skills, learn to create and execute plans and doing their best at whatever projects they tackle.

"To our kids, the state fair is the Super Bowl," Lopez said. "… It doesn't get any bigger than this."

The 4-H and FFA continue to be at the forefront of youth development across the state of Delaware, with much of it due to the dedication of teachers and adult volunteers, he said.

His daughters, Anna and Claire, are active in the Holly Mount 4-H Club and always look forward to the fair. "I do public speaking," said 11-year-old Anna, . "… and I like helping out with my friends sheep."

"I compete with the Horse Bowl," said Claire, two years younger.

Dramatic growth in categories of competition for youngsters – begun with just a handful of livestock categories, limited to boys from Kent and Sussex counties – demonstrates the fair's intense focus on youth development.

There are so many classes of youth competition, in fact, that the fair now creates separate premium books of various sections for 4-H Club and FFA members.

In 4-H, there are now Cloverbud contests for the youngest entrants and a wide variety of sections such as arts and crafts, canning, field crops, conservation, science, sewing, vegetables and woodworking. 4-H Club members from all over Delaware compete in more than 350 classes and contests from public speaking and creating table place settings to archery and tractor driving.

Similarly, the FFA has more than 160 competitive classes in agriculture-related classes including grains, vegetables, shop projects, horticulture/floriculture, dried floral and silk arrangements, shadowboxes, eggs, agriscience fair projects and chapter exhibits. They also compete in career development events.

Open children's competitions also have been enlarged and refined over time to encourage competition and boost recognition in the various departments. Each youngster can enter more than 100 classes in canning, crafts, culinary, drawing and painting, needlepoint, needlework, photography, sewing and woodworking areas. Another group has classes for any knitted, crocheted, hooked or woven articles.

Sections group entrants to compete with youngsters their own age – Section 1 for ages 6 through 9, Section 2 for ages 10 through 12, and Section 3 for ages 13 through 16. Classes also are designated for youngsters with disabilities.

Altogether, there are more than 40,000 competitive entries by young exhibitors every year.

Thousands are animals from rabbits to cattle they have spent all year feeding and tending in anticipation of the fair's various competitive shows, as well as its Youth Livestock Auction and Extravaganza.

"And don't forget all the junior exhibitors and their goats," General Manager Bill DiMondi advised. The Goat Department truly is the "Rodney Dangerfield" of the fair, rarely feeling the love or getting the attention and respect it deserves. Still, the goat department is the fair's single largest livestock department, rightfully boasting an on-grounds census of more than 770 goats, mainly shown by junior exhibitors. But the Goat Department's popularity is growing, perhaps thanks in part to baby goats becoming the darlings of viral internet videos around the world.

Fair organizers keep challenging the youngsters with new contests as part of "keeping it fresh" for young competitors.

Among popular recent additions are shoebox-size miniature "floats" that illustrate the fair's annual slogan, button crafts, decorated jars and creations made out of duct tape.

"It's amazing to see how hard they work on their entries," said one mother who didn't want to be identified because her children might be embarrassed. "I know my kids work on theirs all year and can't wait to come down to the fair and see what ribbon they got."

While they're excited when they win blue ribbons and love the cash premiums they get, she said, getting the red ribbons of second place can be disappointing. But even third-place showings provide good life lessons, she said, and she always encourages them to learn from judges' comments and strive, as the 4-H Motto says, "to Make the Best Better."

Nearly two decades ago, as 4-H and FFA members' entries nearly overflowed their facilities, the fair board made a $4 million investment in what became not only a new exhibition hall but also a community recreational facility.

Now known as The Centre, the building serves as the 4-H and FFA exhibit hall during the fair and, the rest of the year, is a public ice skating rink that meets National Hockey League standards and is available for teams, lessons, events, birthday parties, and private party, meeting or event rental.

Fair leaders consulted with county parks and recreation directors about what was needed in the community and learned that local youth hockey teams and figure skaters of all ages had to travel to Newark or Maryland's Eastern Shore because southern Delaware had no ice rink of its own.

The shortage was so dramatic that existing facilities were crammed to the point that local teams were switching from ice hockey to roller hockey because they couldn't get ice time, Randy Hooker, then the fair's marketing director, said as the plan was announced in 2000.

"The construction allows us to fulfill the recreational needs of southern Delaware in a truly unique way as well as keep our focus on agriculture and education – all within the confines of one big building," said Bill DiMondi, who was then fair president and now is general manager. He also introduced a popular new feature at The Centre, ice bumper cars, after seeing the attraction at a rink while on vacation in Colorado.

FUN ON ICE

A wild idea journeyed nearly 2,000 miles in 2017 to become a tremendously popular feature at a special building on the fairgrounds.

That's the multi-purpose Centre.

During the fair, it's the exhibit hall for 4-H and FAA members' entries in a wide array of classes, also hosting many displays and demonstration programs.

The rest of the year, it's an ice rink and program facility.

"Bumper Cars on Ice" arrived there from the only place they were found in the United States – Howelsen Ice Arena, a municipal complex in Steamboat Springs, Colorado – thanks to the fair's General Manager Bill DiMondi.

DiMondi was on vacation when he was intrigued by an advertisement for the bumper cars and had to see them for himself – and he did.

"I knew we had to have them," DiMondi said.

The bumper cars – built by the rink's maintenance manager Mike Farney with motorized wheels and joy stick controls – are plenty popular in Colorado and boost overall use of the rink by skaters. DiMondi made a deal to buy 10 of them, getting the bumper cars at cost as Farney eyed the start of his own international import company. His idea is to get frames, motors and high-tech controls from China for installation in fiberglass tub bodies made in Colorado, so he was quite interested to see how the bumper cars might go over in Delaware.

DiMondi said he figured they would be a natural fit and nice addition for The Centre Ice Rink, a feature that adds greatly to the fairgrounds' year-round use.

From mid-August to mid-June, the 49,000-square-foot rink is open to the public, with an National Hockey League regulation-size ice surface, seating for 350 spectators including a heated viewing lobby, hockey and figure-skating lessons, party and meeting rooms, video arcade, snack bar and pro shop.

Before The Centre's creation, local hockey players had to travel more than an hour to play.

Since its opening in October 2002, the fair-owned site has been offering a unique community venue not only for skating but also for rental for birthday parties, large dinner events, meetings, dinners and other events.

Still, when "Bumper Cars on Ice" opened there in September 2017, the public reaction surprised even DiMondi.

Not only did more than 400 people line up to ride them that weekend, "Bumper Cars on Ice" made a big media splash.

"It really was a blast," Kim Abner of Federalsburg, Maryland, told The News Journal. The newspaper featured two full pages with its story and color photos about the debut of the bumper cars-on-ice, even including an "If You Go" box with details and referral to delawarestatefairgrounds.com for more information. The News Journal Media Group also posted the coverage online.

"That's probably the best coverage we've ever gotten in The News Journal," DiMondi said.

And the state fair video went viral.

"It's amazing," said Danny Aguilar, the fair's assistant general manager and director of marketing.

In less than two weeks, the video racked up 750,000+ views.

AN ADVENTURE LAND

For generations, the entire fair setting has been an adventure land for younger fairgoers, often seen exploring on their own with friends – and parents' permission and blessing.

"It's always been the kind of place where parents could go with older kids and say, 'Have a good time and let's meet at the front gate at such-and-such time.' You can feel comfortable when you turn your kids loose and not worry about them," said Peter C. Schwartzkopf, whose perspective on the fair is multi-faceted.

Schwartzkopf served at the fair as a Delaware State Police trooper and, later, as the fair's security director. Now, as Speaker of the Delaware House of Representatives, the Rehoboth Beach Democrat is a solid supporter of the fair at the state capital and sees its benefits from economics to instilling a sense of place with the kind of values in young people that help make the state strong.

The fair is an incredible asset for Delaware, he said, adding its impact reaches far beyond being a well-earned source of pride and an enduring economic force.

"It's wholesome, it's all-American and it's safe," he said. "It's a great place for our kids, our grandchildren and our great-grandchildren to have a little independence when they're old enough to start running around with their friends and enjoy the games."

"We're lucky to have the Delaware State Fair," he added, "and I hope we have it for another 100 years … or more."

In addition to all the fun from rides and animals to attractions and competition geared to young people, he noted, the fair exposes children to future possibilities from careers in agriculture to law enforcement.

And while he recalls that state police uniforms of his era were wool that was far too warm at fair time, Schwartzkopf said, "I was one of the troopers who always loved being at the fair."

And their presence continues to be popular with the younger generations.

As the nightly parade progressed across the fairgrounds one evening, a mother and son stood transfixed, watching the entourage of farm machinery and marchers.

"Look, Daniel!" the mother exclaimed as a remote-controlled Tyrannosaurus rex ambled into view. "A dinosaur!"

"No, Mom," he replied. "Look at the horse police!"

And soon he joined a group of happy children, reaching up to pet the smiling troopers' big beasts.

DEVELOPING YOUNG LEADERS

Aside from enjoying the classic aspects of the fair itself, youngsters also are encouraged to be involved in the Delaware State Fair Junior Board, teen volunteering and annual Childen's Day, with free admission for everyone 12 or younger and a schedule of special activities and contests throughout the day.

The Junior Board offers six positions for 16- through 21-year-olds who serve two-year terms, developing leadership skills through their participation. In addition to spending at least 30 hours of volunteer time before and during the fair, members learn about what goes into presenting the fair each year.

Hannah O'Hara of Milford, a longtime member of the Houston Cardinals 4-H Club, said she got involved in the state fair as part of the 4-H State Teen Council, joining a meet-and-greet with U.S. Secretary of Agriculture George Ervin "Sonny" Perdue III.

By the age of 17, she had annual projects including archery, public speaking, citizenship, science, food and nutrition, photography and horticulture. And she was in the habit of having scores of state fair entries every year, as many as 75 in classes from wildlife to consumer finance.

"The state fair is really incredible and it's a big part of my life," she said, adding that her sister Shannon, three years younger, also is an enthusiastic 4-Her with almost as many annual fair entries as she has.

They love planning and creating their entries, then seeing them on display at the fair – not to mention the substantial premium money they both earn.

But being part of the Junior Board, Hannah said, has given her a unique, behind-the-scenes understanding of all the hard work, caring and coordination it takes to make the fair a fun experience – for all ages of fairgoers. Her work varied from helping prepare for and hold events to checking in entries, placing campers and helping judges scan entry tags and place ribbons. "It takes all year round to make sure this is up and running," she said with a big smile. "It's a lot of work … and it's all worth it."

OUR ACTIVE YOUTH

Many Delaware State Fair directors and volunteers past and present can trace their early connection with the event to youthful years as members of 4-H Clubs and Future Farmers of America, now known simply as FFA.

And that connection is not a thing of the past.

It's a growing trend.

The fair, which provides hundreds of competitions and other opportunities, has been cited as one of the factors helping both youth organizations thrive in the state.

FFA, begun in 1928 – dedicated to developing youth leadership potential, personal growth and agriculture-science education for career success – boasts record statewide membership of 4,200.

A wide variety of 4-H programs statewide have been estimated as reaching some 70,000 young people – or nearly half of those eligible, The News Journal reported in 2014.

With that figure including after-school programs, the tally counts the federally sponsored program's participation rate more than twice that of any other state.

The 4-H program, which became national in 1914, focuses on four personal, leadership and life-skill development areas – Head, Heart, Hands, Health – also emphasizing citizenship, community responsibility and global impact.

And Delaware has been cited as the First State of 4-H, with the highest per capita participation in the United States.

Top right: Governor John Carney and 4-Hers

EXTRAORDINARY 4-HER

A plaque at The Centre honors a state fair pioneer and national leader who first came to the fairgrounds as a young 4-Her aiming for blue ribbons.

Joy Lynn Gooden Sparks, who grew up in Kent County and later lived in Newark and Dewey Beach, went from earning blue ribbons to making 4-H her life's work. Later, the state fair would name a memorial tribute award in her honor.

Over 35 years as a 4-H agent through University of Delaware's Cooperative Extension Service, she was a driving force for youth development, helping build the Delaware 4-H Club Program into a national powerhouse.

She led the youth leadership and development organization to grow in membership and staffing, with state and federal support. Sparks also helped the group grow into non-traditional areas, such as the 4-H Military Partnership with Dover Air Force Base and the Delaware National Guard. She also played a major role in establishing the Delaware 4-H Foundation, which raised $300,000 in its first campaign, coordinated to the 100th anniversary of 4-H.

Also active in other nonprofit groups, Sparks won many state- and national-level awards and recognitions from her alma mater University of Delaware, the National Association of Extension 4-H Agents, Delaware Farm Bureau, Delaware 4-H Foundation and numerous other organizations.

In 1988, she became a director of the Delaware State Fair and was the first woman to have the distinction of serving on the executive committee as one of the fair's vice presidents.

Before Sparks died 2009 at age 57 after battling cancer, Delaware – then reaching nearly 70,000 youngsters or more than 47 percent of eligible children – was recognized as the state with the highest per capita 4-H participation in the United States.

And she was recognized as one of the main forces behind that national achievement.

PLAYING POLITICS

ONE OF THE oldest traditions of the Delaware State Fair is Governor's Day, when people of the state – or anywhere else – get the chance to meet, greet and share a little face time with the top office-holder.

Governor's Day, a concept that began with one of the state fair's predecessors as "Politicians Day," also provides a time for those in or seeking any level of elective office to reach out to voters.

Among other things, it's been a time in recent years for Governor John Carney to meet prize-winning chickens, for Governor Jack Markell to enjoy the egg-toss, for Governor Tom Carper to ride the bumper cars and for Governor Mike Castle to play Whac-a-Mole.

"It's pretty special," said Carney, who regards the fair as a treasured tradition of "our way of life and our agricultural heritage… This is a tremendous fair."

"Look, look!" a woman squealed as

On facing page: Governor Ruth Ann Minner
Center: Governor Sherman Tribbett

he rode up on a golf cart. "It's the governor!"

She and others rushed over to meet Carney, who blushed a bit at her announcement of his arrival.

"I'd have to say that Governor's Day is my favorite part of the fair, now that I've been elected," Lieutenant Governor Bethany Hall-Long said as she spent the day there with Carney. But she added with a laugh, "when I was younger, my favorite part was the rides."

She joined Governor Carney on a barn tour that saw them both holding chickens and chatting with exhibitors of all ages from throughout the state. Carney also has been joined for days at the fair by his wife, Delaware First Lady Tracey Carney, who has attended a variety of events, programs and tours, also helping present numerous awards.

The Governor's Day Dinner is unique as the only major fair event held at the Harrington Raceway on the fairgrounds. Presented by Blue Cross Blue Shield Delaware, the event features a cocktail hour, dinner, presentation of the governor and live harness racing.

"It's always a special event," said Ron Draper, fair president.

One longtime politician, who said he couldn't take credit by name for the age-old description, called Governor's Day "a time for movers and shakers and state lawmakers."

In 1932, Governor C. Douglass Buck's arrival at the fair was greeted with a 21-gun salute.

In 1946, Governor Walter W. Bacon called attending Governor's Day "a delightful privilege."

A front-page article in the Wilmington Morning News said Bacon "lauded the contribution the fair makes to the vast agricultural industry of Delaware, mentioning in particular that it gives agriculturists an opportunity to meet, compare equipment and methods, and study their problems." He also said he was pleased "to bring the state's greetings to the fair officers, directors and managers in tribute to their perseverance over the years in presenting so successful a program of interest not only to the farmer but to the city dweller as well."

Within a few more years, Governor's Day publicly was being called a day when "everyone wants to be seen and heard."

Top: left to right: Governors Elbert N. Carvel, Walter W. Bacon, J. Caleb Boggs, John G. Townsend Jr.

Center: Governor J. Caleb Boggs with Smokey Bear, Delaware Forestry Commission Chairman Willard Springer Jr.

Bottom: Governor Elbert N. Carvel and family

By the 1950s, Governor's Day was considered "the place to unofficially begin the fall political campaigns for both parties," one news account said.

But the 1952 fair lacked both the governor and lieutenant governor – Elbert N. Carvel and Alexis I. du Pont Bayard, respectively – at its Governor's Day celebration because a last-minute program change by the National Democratic Convention in Chicago required their attendance there.

The attorney general designated as acting governor filled in but so did former U.S. Senator John G. Townsend Jr., himself a former Delaware governor.

His term as governor notably included signing legislation that established the fair. He also won local hearts in his brief remarks that Governor's Day, saying, "I've traveled many parts of the world but I have never found a better place than the three counties – Sussex, Kent and New Castle – of Delaware."

In 1954, Governor J. Caleb Boggs introduced three of his predecessors – Townsend, Bacon and Carvel – but shifted the focus from the state's top job to those who chose the person for that office. "I think of this as a day honoring all of the citizens of Delaware," he said.

In his day, the traditional Governor's Day dinner was much more intimate. Boggs was served in a private Pennsylvania Railroad dining car that was side-tracked to downtown Harrington for the occasion, with guests then driving to the fair in by car in a caravan.

Begun as a time to "salute and entertain the First Citizen," as one early news account said, the day was evolving in the 1960s and 1970s into more of an occasion for the governor to "work the fair."

That became especially the case starting with modern-era governors such as Russell W. Peterson, Sherman Tribbitt and Pete du Pont, as different organizations within the fair began hosting more events specifically for Governor's Day, such as the watermelon-eating contest and crowd-pleasing egg toss.

"Governor's Day is always special," said Andrew West, editor of the Delaware State News, which takes rightful pride in its extensive coverage of the fair every year. Delaware's governors tend to be good sports, he said. But nowhere is that truer than at the fair, where fairgoers' selfies and media interviews, photos and videos forever preserve their day.

And while governors in most-recent decades tend to attend the fair on several days, more than their designated day, is filled by activities from morning through night, with the grand finale of the whole day's shebang being the Governor's Day Dinner. And while it's fine – even expected – for the governor to carry exhaustion and sunburn of the long day by then, the dinner gathers an uncommonly influential audience and includes one of the state's top horse racing events.

Indeed, the event fills the raceway's Clubhouse Dining Room with a Who's Who of Delaware and plenty of patriotic spirit – including presentation of colors by the Delaware National Guard and a rousing rendition of The Star-Spangled Banner.

At one recent dinner, both Major General (Retired) Francis D. Vavala, former Adjutant General of the State of Delaware, and his successor Major General Carol A. Timmons, thanked the fair for its Military Appreciation Day and warm reception of military families.

Applause for them and the historic Delaware National Guard – with roots back to 1655, when Swedish settlers served as militia defending the New Sweden colony – was both thunderous and sustained.

After a hearty and elegant dinner, cheers rose again, with another standing ovation until the horses crossed the finish line.

Governor's Day is the richest day of the year in Delaware harness racing, with 100 percent of entries either Delaware-owned or Delaware-bred, which means prize money stays within the state, along with the special bragging rights for the winner of the popular Governor's Cup race.

"We're so lucky to have this fair," said Delaware State Representative Paul Baumbach of Newark, while attending the dinner event with his wife Pam, also a self-proclaimed "big fan of the fair."

"A lot of people don't understand how they work all year to make the fair such a great event," he added.

Governor's Day is a time of good sportsmanship and plenty of handshaking, even for elected officials in positions other than the state's top executive – and more than a few candidates who saw themselves competing for the same offices.

Especially in election years, it's a campaigning spot few statewide or southern Delaware office candidates are willing to risk missing.

A newspaper editorial in advance of the 1931 fair noted that "Really there is a niche in our scheme of things that only a fair can fill. The fair affords the only real opportunity there is for the people from all parts of the State to meet and renew acquaintance; to gather together for pleasure once a year.

"It is the only recognized Mecca for politicians of all parties. Many a ticket for the ensuing election has been 'fixed up' at the state fair, and we are not sure that something of the kind will not happen at Harrington this week."

But Governor's Day goes far beyond trying to get support or votes in the next election, officials say.

It provides an important opportunity to connect with a large number of people coming from all over the state, to hear any concerns or problems they might have and to thank them for the privilege of serving in public office.

And some do get an earful.

"I like the chance to get my message to elected officials," said Al Thompson of Norwood, Pennsylvania.

Thompson typically staffs a fair space for the small business he owns, but also carries two other business cards. One promotes his work as editor-in-chief of an online magazine called "footballstories" and sports director for WRDV Radio 89.3 FM, while the other card is strictly for his nonprofit organization, "Protect Our Youth from Steroids."

When he's not at his business booth, Thompson said he enjoys spreading the word about youth sports and the dangers of steroids, while lobbying for restrictions to prevent their use and abuse.

Delaware's elected officials "have been very receptive," he said.

Other highlights of Governor's Day include fair tours with Delaware Secretary of Agriculture Michael Scuse, welcoming firefighters home from battling wildfires across the country, recognizing anniversaries such as the Delaware Weatherization Program's 40th year and drawing the winning ticket in the Division of Motor Vehicles' raffle of a black-and-white Delaware license plate.

Above: Governor Elbert N. Carvel

Carney said one of his favorite moments was meeting a man who had been attending the fair – and exhibiting – for 80 years.

"Can you imagine?" Carney said.

And when the honoree said he was honored to meet the governor, Carney said the honor was all his.

"He was amazing," said Carney, who said he could not have been more impressed by one person's lifelong involvement in the fair.

Later that day, speaking at the Governor's Day Dinner, Carney said "this has been a great day," adding that part of the reason why was that he got to spend the whole day with his wife.

But he added, "It's not about the governor, it's really not. And it shouldn't be…. It's about the young people."

He grew reflective, recalling a former governor calling Delaware "a state of neighbors" and said he had to concur. "We don't always agree, but at the end of the day, we do what's right for our state."

And, in a once-in-a-lifetime moment of Governor's Day at the 99th annual Delaware State Fair, Carney signed a unique piece of legislation.

The measure authorizes the state's creation of what is expected to become the ultimate collectible among Delaware State Fair souvenirs: Official license plates issued by the state, commemorating the fair centennial.

GOVERNOR'S STAND-IN

In 1952, the attorney general filled in on Governor's Day at the fair.

Governor Elbert N. Carvel had planned to attend, but the Democratic National Convention changed its schedule, forcing him and Lieutenant Governor Alexis I. du

Above: Governor Mike Castle

Pont Bayard to cancel their plans to go to Harrington and head instead to the Chicago convention.

Attorney General H. Albert Young was serving in their absence as acting governor, including in the role they could not fill at the fair. After praising winners of the beauty competition that was part of the Delmarva Chicken Festival at the fair and congratulating fair officials on the event's success, he noted that the fair, having passed the 30-year mark, had "become the principal event of its kind in the annual history of our state."

The rest of his remarks from the open, sun-lit platform across from the main grandstands, must have been poignant considering the end just years earlier of World War II and bear repeating:

Bottom: Governor Jack Markell

173

"For variety of exhibits, for number of participants, for the interest it creates in the agricultural development of our state, it ranks now with the other great fairs that are annual fixtures in the Eastern United States.

"More than that, this fair brings home to each one of us the ties we have with the good earth. For no matter how removed from the farm and the soil we may be in our daily occupations and in the avocations that fill our spare time, each one of us is indebted finally for our basic needs to the soil.

"Each one of us in turn owes his good health and the fact that he is able to prosper, whatever his business or profession or trade, to the farmer whose never-ending toil brings magic in the form of food from this good earth.

"And what does this fair signify to us as we return here to Harrington year after year?

"To me it means that the magicians of the soil are proud of their achievements and are happy to bring them here for us to see. It means another year has brought new progress from the fields and the pens and that there are new things to see. It means that those of us, especially you men and women who have organized and managed these fairs, year after year, are conscious of our debt to the fertile soil of our great land.

Above: Governor Tom Carper

"It means, too, that here we have, brought together, an example of the abundant life of the United States. Here we see man and nature cooperating, industry and agriculture working side by side, finance complementing ingenuity.

"Because we are a nation composed of millions of men and women to whom the good earth is a challenge and because we have been wonderfully blessed with arable land, we are the hope and arsenal of decent peoples of the world.

"From our farms come the foods that help sustain the armies that are protecting these peoples. From our farms come strong young men fighting with these armies of democracy.

"From our agricultural wonderland we derive the national strength that fires all of us the world over to great deeds.

"May we gather here together for years to come in a world of peace and security."

ON PARADE

THE FAIR'S NIGHTLY parade is like something from a Norman Rockwell painting, an old-fashioned, all-American procession that smiling spectators join to share the fun.

"That's one of our oldest fair traditions," said LeRoy Betts, a fair director and past president. "It's like an old hometown parade, really, but it runs through the fair grounds."

And it's different every night of every year, except that there's a longstanding and continuing presence of antique tractors and farm equipment, troopers from the Delaware State Police, some kind of family-friendly music and, prominently displayed, plenty of American flags.

Depending on the night, there also may be floats and vintage cars, decorated golf carts, a noisy gaggle of loud antique tractors, robotic dinosaurs, and popular cartoon characters like Peppa Pig, strolling along with musicians, magicians and puppeteers.

Each nightly parade is led by State Senator and Fair Director Dave Wilson and two of the most beautiful horse-drawn carriages to be seen anywhere. In addition to volunteering his own time, the senator provides the skills of a second carriage driver for each night's parade. Special guests of the fair and the "youth of the day" – along with his or her immediate family members – are featured prominently in each of the horse drawn carriages.

The parade also is a prime venue for high school and community bands throughout Delaware and many performers find time to join the march between their fair shows.

Many first-time spectators are quick to notice the required clean-up crews equipped with extremely wide shovels that follow the Delaware State Police Mounted Patrol Unit and other animals in the parade that may leave manure in their wake – a reality known to make some young spectators cheer or howl with delight.

"Look!" one little girl squealed, clapping her hands. "That horsie just made big poopies!"

The fun steps off nightly at 7 from The Centre Ice Rink/4-H and FFA Building, strolls past the Grandstands down Williams Street, runs around the Quillen Arena to Holloway Street, then heads back to its starting point.

Although that covers a lot of ground – and brings the parade to about 5,000 or so fairgoers – the march typically runs just under half an hour. Keeping it short and sweet makes it a perfect family event, suitable even for youngsters with short attention spans.

KENT & SUSSEX FAIR

OPENS
MONDAY
JULY 23rd

6 DAYS
6 NIGHTS

HARRINGTON
DEL.
37th ANNUAL

IRISH HORAN
HELL DRIVERS
ALL NEW FOR '56
ONE NIGHT ONLY
THE SHOW ALIVE WITH DEATH

CHILDREN'S DAY
TUESDAY
SPECIAL ATTRACTIONS
ALL SCHOOL CHILDREN
ADMITTED FREE

GOVERNOR'S DAY
THURSDAY

GIANT LIVESTOCK
PARADE

HARNESS RACING
AND
THRILLING ACTS
MON.-TUES.-WED.-THURS.
PONY RACES

AUTO RACES
FRIDAY & SATURDAY

FIREWORKS
NIGHTLY

PAT BOONE
FRIDAY NIGHT

MIDWESTERN HAYRIDE
SAT. NIGHT

★ ★ ★ "FANTASIES OF 1956" ★ ★ ★
presenting THE ROXYETTES
50-ARTISTS-50 The Shore's Biggest Event in '56
EVERY AFTERNOON
COMPLETE CHANGE
OF PROGRAM
10 ACTS of VAUDEVILLE and
MAMMOTH REVUE EVERY NIGHT

BASILE'S
MADISON SQUARE
GARDEN BAND

IT HAS EVERYTHING

4-H
& F.F.A.
EXHIBITS

COME TO
THE FAIR

PRELL'S BROADWAY SHOWS
ON THE MIDWAY
SHOWS
RIDES

EXHIBITS OF
FARM MACHINERY
AGRICULTURE
LIVE STOCK
POULTRY
EDUCATION

★ DELAWARE'S BIGGEST OUTDOOR SHOW ★
JULY 23-24-25-26-27-28

FAMILY TREASURES

IN ADVANCE OF the Delaware State Fair Centennial, a public call went out:

Do you have fair souvenirs or memorabilia to share?

Morgan Roberts of Davidsonville, Maryland, was just a 16-year-old kid when he worked at the fair's 1966 concert by Gary Lewis & the Playboys.

That would be the son of comedian Jerry Lewis, who had just skyrocketed to pop music fame as the front man of Gary Lewis & the Playboys, with the first of their string of national Top 40 hits, "This Diamond Ring."

The heartthrob and his bandmates were only a few years older than Roberts was, but they drove the teens wild after appearing on television programs including American Bandstand, Hullaballoo, Shindig and the Ed Sullivan Show.

But more than 50 years later, Roberts came across his somewhat worn souvenir of that day – Stage Pass Number 026 – complete with the barely legible, ballpoint-pen autograph of that day's superstar.

And, having heard that the state fair was about to celebrate its centennial and welcomed loans and donations of memorabilia, Roberts sent along his stage pass. He was among dozens of donors who responded with heart and generosity, sharing family treasures from fairs throughout the century.

"It's amazing to see everything people have contributed," said Administrative Assistant Rebekkah Conley, while eyeing piled-high tables at the fair's Administration Building.

Donations ranged from a glass tile souvenir painting, done by an artist at a booth under the now-enclosed grandstands, to photos, postcards, signs, buttons, programs, banners and more.

A few contributions even predated the modern Delaware State Fair, such as a ruby glass vase from one of the earlier, short-lived fairs that once went by the same name.

Others included albums, photographs, newspaper clippings, ribbons and fair premium books.

All loaned items were being photographed or copied, Conley said, while donations became part of the permanent Delaware State Fair collection to be shared with the public in a variety of displays.

Many of the items were selected for display at a special Delaware State Fair Centennial exhibit at the Delaware Public Archives.

In addition to those whose loans or donations are pictured here, both the Delaware State Fair and Delaware Public Archives thank everyone who responded for their heartfelt generosity.

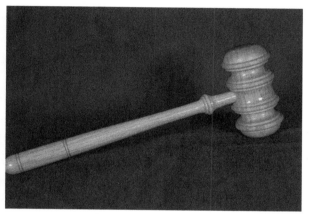

VIEW FROM ABOVE

THE FOOTPRINT OF the Delaware State Fairgrounds at Harrington has grown through the acquisition of adjoining lands large and small, with several purchases from families that were honored to have their land help their beloved fair grow.

These aerial photos, starting with the earliest-known overhead image – taken during the sixth annual fair – show the growth, new buildings and increased parking area through the years.

There's a saying that real estate is all about three things: "Location, location and location."

Perhaps proof of the success of Delaware State Fair's Harrington site is that the event is the only one of three fairs to use the statewide name that didn't move or go bankrupt.

The first to use the name began at Canterbury in the late 1800s, moved to Dover and ended in 1901.

In 1901, a totally separate Delaware State Fair started in Wilmington. That one moved to Elsmere in 1917, but closed seven years later.

187

First-known aerial view, 1926

1948

Circa 1970s with clubhouse addition to the grandstands

Modern-day view from above

THE GROWING FAIRGROUNDS

1. Original fair site
   30 acres
   Purchased from William S. Smith
   February 17, 1920

2. Tharp property
   5,200 square feet, highway access
   Acquired March 21, 1921

3. Thistlewood property
   40 acres
   Acquired September 16, 1925

4. J G. & Elva Smith property
   10 acres
   Acquired May 10, 1930

5. Gill property
   3 acres
   Acquired September 12, 1939

6. Tharp property
   3 acres
   Acquired September 12, 1939

7. Billings property
   35 acres
   Acquired October 21, 1950

8. Von Goerres property
   80 acres
   Acquired October 3, 1962

9. Billings Estate property
   21 acres
   Acquired July 2, 1964

10. Frankhouser Property
    38 acres
    Acquired November 13, 1964

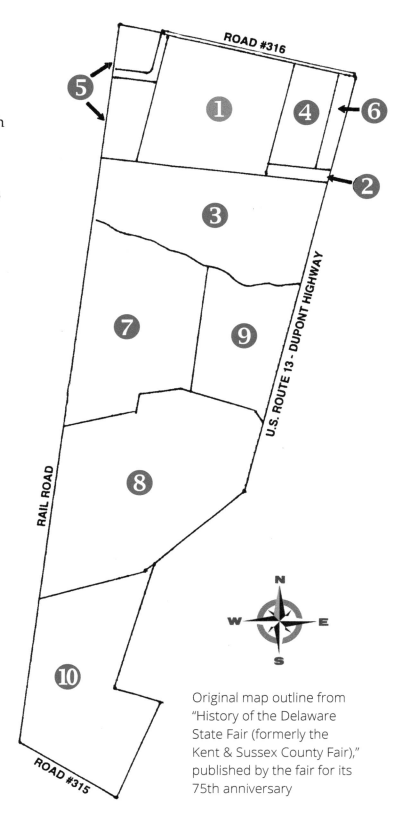

Original map outline from "History of the Delaware State Fair (formerly the Kent & Sussex County Fair)," published by the fair for its 75th anniversary

Up in the Air

Helicopter rides instantly became one of the most popular new features at the fair, giving fairgoers their first opportunities to take their own aerial photographs and videos.

The one-of-a-kind rides attract a steady stream of fairgoers, eager to see the promised "best view of the fairgrounds."

The thuck-thuck-thuck sound of blades drew both the curious and determined to the flight area, safely cleared and designated near the main gate.

All helicopter rides at the fair begin there with a safety briefing and, usually, end with grinning faces and photos posted on social media.

Kyle Grantham, then a News Journal photographer, even shared his view from the helicopter on a bright and sunny Friday at the 2015 fair in a special feature by the newspaper and website called "First State Focus."

And for those who love the bright lights at night, rides provided by Charm City Helicopters at the 2018 fair offered prime viewing from the sky all the way to 11 p.m.

For many of the passengers at the fair, the ride also marks their first time in a helicopter.

With the fairgrounds easily viewable, the rides can be kept far less expensive than going up in a big-city helicopter tour or joining a charter flight that could cost hundreds of more.

"I can't wait," one man said as he dashed toward the launch area. "I've been looking forward to this since I saw the helicopter last year."

Tickets were a bargain for the once-in-a-lifetime experience of nonstop fun and excitement – and such a wonderful shared memory – that the Delaware mother-daughter duo of Loretta and Ava Getty never will forget.

They had such a tremendous time, they were happy to share their pictures for this book, for the souvenir photos of their enjoyment and appreciation to become part of the permanent history of the Delaware State Fair.

And when the helicopter finally whirred slowly and touched down onto the fairgrounds, the little girl's reaction was priceless.

"Can we go again, Mom?"

SAFE SKIES

A popular trend prompted a relatively new safety rule that earlier generations could not have imagined.

The sky above the Delaware State Fairgrounds has been declared a "No-Drone Zone."

Until recent years, dictionary definitions of "drone" tended to be limited to the verb for making a low humming noise and noun for that sound, some male bees and lackluster human workers. But that was before advancing modern technology prompted plunging prices and resulting popularization of small, remote-controlled aircraft, often equipped with cameras.

"Love them or hate them," TechRepublic said in 2018, "drones are here to stay."

The tech service's article went on to detail what it called "17 drone disasters that show why the FAA hates drones." They ranged from a 2014 drone mishap that cut off the tip of a New York photographer's nose to the 2015 crash of a drone packed with drugs and a drone crash in 2017, smack into Seattle's famous Space Needle.

Out of an abundance of caution – and before any mishaps took place – fair leaders officially designated the fairgrounds as a "No Drone Zone."

Those who want aerial photos can buy tickets for the fair's helicopter rides. Otherwise, the use of any drone or aerial equipment for any purpose, whether for personal posting or advertising, requires advance authorization in writing – directly from the fair – as a precautionary safety measure to protect all the people and animals on the ground, as well as fair buildings, fairgoers' vehicles and other property.

FAIR WEATHER

Delaware State Fair's timing puts the event in one of the year's warmest and most humid times, prone to summer storms. But the seasonal weather is a variable fair organizers know to expect.

"Heat and rain can always affect attendance," said Danny Aguilar, assistant general manager and director of marketing.

And, like the Wilmington Flower Market always seems to get rain on its Mother's Day Weekend, the fair seems to get a heat wave, downpour or both.

"Heat over 100 will keep the crowd down," he said, "more than rain will."

Many fairgoers prepare for a bit of rain – and enjoy it, he said.

Since the fair invested more than $1 million on blacktop and concrete paving over a period of many years, dust and mud no longer create problems along the roads and carnival grounds.

During hotter and more-humid fairs, organizers make sure there are

197

plenty of places to cool off, including popular walk-through misting stations. And, unlike early years before fair buildings had air conditioning, they make sure to keep inside temperatures refreshingly low – with plenty of fans, water hoses and hand-held sprayers to cool animals.

Exhibitors' freebies also reflect the weather – with fans plentiful in heat and ponchos popular in rain.

The University of Delaware has even studied fair weather, placing an "environmental observing station" on the fairgrounds near the race track.

In 2011, only two fair days dropped below 90 degrees and the 96-degree opening day had high humidity that made it feel like 107. Then, on July 22 that year, the recorded high was 101.7 degrees with a heat index of 117.3.

That made the fair the hottest since the UD station began keeping statistics.

Weather was positively gentle by comparison in 2013 and 2014. UD recorded the lowest high of 83.3 degrees on July 25, 2013, and the lowest low of 58 degrees on July 18, 2014.

The rainiest fair day on record was July 21, 2018, with a drenching 5.25 inches. Before that, it was July 22, 2006, with a mere 1.4 inches.

A little rain usually doesn't deter fairgoers and is to be expected, fair officials say.

While details about the weather are limited from the fair's early years, a few drops of rain in 1968 have become a thing of legend.

That year, Smokey Robinson was booked as the big act at the height of his popularity – and the show quickly sold out.

The singer and his group were late arriving at the fairgrounds, where light rain began to fall as the crowd waited for him to go on.

Then, as the story goes, the star reportedly stuck his hand out of his dressing room door, felt a few drops and canceled the show.

Another year, rain was welcomed, although not especially on the fairgrounds.

Delaware was suffering a long and intense drought, raising concerns about dramatically low water levels in the Brandywine, Red Clay and White Clay creeks, as well as crop damage, including corn drying on the stalk in the state's farm fields when it was supposed to be tasseling.

State officials gathered to discuss the increasingly critical drought and were on the verge of declaring a state of emergency.

Then one official reminded the group that the state fair was to open the next week.

As if on cue, rain began as the fair opened and fell all week.

In 1962, a sudden storm tore tents, blew away signs and toppled a double Ferris wheel, but cooperation and swift repairs followed quickly.

And, one night in 2018, the possibility of lightning in a thunderstorm prompted a precautionary early closure.

Back in 1997, when country artist Vince Gill was performing on stage, the sky turned an angry black color and a Category 1 tornado passed just west of the fairgrounds – before leveling commercial buildings in Felton.

But the fair goes on.

And despite both heat and rain for the 99th annual fair, attendance was up 2 percent from the previous year, at 291,316.

More notable, however, is that the weather didn't stop the fair from setting a new record for the top one-day attendance in its history, with a count of 48,653 on Saturday, July 28.

At dusk, the crowd pouring onto the grounds was as energized and big – or bigger than – a typical opening day of the fair.

With a nice night and plenty going on, it seemed everyone who put off coming to the fair because of the heat or rain decided to come on closing day.

"It was amazing," DiMondi said.

And that warm summer night made fair history.

But fair organizers hope to set more attendance records with the 100th anniversary fair in 2019.

At a planning meeting for that special occasion, one director kept a straight face – but got a big laugh – as he announced in a somewhat formal manner that he wanted to inform the group he officially filed a formal request, more than a year in advance, regarding the centennial fair.

For it to have perfect weather.

A SPECIAL EYE: THE BENNETT GALLERY

Uncounted thousands of people have taken pictures at the Delaware State Fair, but none could outdo Robert J. Bennett of Bridgeville, whose dedication and duration led to his being named as the fair's first official photographer – a title created for the longtime role he already filled.

Service in the U.S. Army led to Bennett developing his talents as a professional photographer.

His career behind the camera began in the U.S. Army Signal Corps, serving in Germany from 1951 to 1953 as an Army photographer, and continued through his passing in 2006 at the age of 76.

Bennett's photographs appeared in publications around the world, winning many awards and honors.

He also had a long career with the U.S. Postal Service, starting in 1945, with positions as postmaster in Dover and Rehoboth Beach before his retirement in 1984.

He served as president of the Delaware Postmasters Association and was an officer of the National Postmasters Association.

Bennett, devoted to community, was a member of the Bridgeville Volunteer Fire Company for more than

50 years, serving as president in 1956, and served in the Delaware Fire Police.

In addition, he served on the Bridgeville Town Commission, was director of the Bridgeville Historical Society and was an active member in the Bridgeville Lions Club, Bridgeville Kiwanis Club, Rehoboth Art League, Seaford Golf and Country Club, Union United Methodist Church and the board of Nanticoke Health Services. In his spare time, he was an avid stamp collector, specializing in first day covers.

As a longtime fan of the Delaware State Fair, he began taking pictures there long before he became a member of the board in 1993. He captured many unique behind-the-scenes images of construction crews, employees, vendors and livestock, as well as classic fair time shots of folks of all ages enjoying the annual event – from popcorn to the Pretty Animal Contest.

Over many years, Bennett already was filling the role long before being named as the fair's first official photographer. He also traveled the state, photographing farms, farmers and other subjects, but remained the fair photographer until the day he died..

That July, the Delaware State Fair Board of Directors honored him by creating the Bob Bennett Photo Gallery in the Judges Chambers, citing his "remarkable contribution."

Amid the images that line the walls, a plaque with a photo of him and his camera says in part that "it was not unusual to see Bob, with his trusty camera strapped around his neck, traversing the grounds in pursuit of that perfect shot to memorialize and event or scene during Fair Week."

Eleanor Bennett – his wife of more than 50 years, also a fair volunteer – honored and preserved his photography, donating his work to the people through the state archives in Dover.

"The Delaware Public Archives is incredibly fortunate to be the recipient of Ms. Bennett's generous donation of her husband's photo collection," said Corey Marshall-Steele, the archives' marketing/exhibits manager and public information officer.

"With a remarkable eye, he captured scenes of farming and agricultural life over more than half a century," he said. "His work as the first official photographer of the Delaware State Fair also is outstanding.

"The Robert J. Bennett Photograph Collection is a remarkable asset that the archives will preserve and share," Marshall-Steele added. "His thousands of artful and engaging images are a timeless treasure that will help tell the story of Delaware life to current and future generations."

1990 DELA. STATE FAIR
JULY 19th to 28th
BARBARA MANDRELL ★ MILLI VANILLI ★
RANDY TRAVIS ★ SHOT GUN RED ★
THE YOUNG & THE RESTLESS STARS ★
RICKY VAN SHELTON & K.T. OSLIN ★

SIGNS OF THE TIMES

At The Social Spot – a real sign-of-the-times at the Delaware State Fair – teenage volunteers staffing the area chuckled at the idea of what the fair founders of a century ago might think of their technology from Facebook to selfies.

"Probably, they'd think it was magic," said Maycee Collison, 16, of Harrington, a member of the Harrington Sunshine 4-H Club.

"Or voodoo," said Elle Wood, also a 16-year-old from Harrington, but a member of the Peach Blossom 4-H Club.

Otherwise, the girls agreed, how would the fair's founders explain a selfie?

The Social Spot – for "all things social media at the fair" – was established in 2017 and immediately became a popular feature in the Exhibit Hall.

There, fairgoers could take their own cell phone photos using provided frames or have their pictures made and featured by the fair on social media. Their photos also are displayed for other fairgoers to see.

Here, fairgoers also have the fun of becoming part of the news by going live with media personalities broadcasting on radio and television.

Displays posted their photos for other fairgoers — and all Social Spot visitors left with prizes from polo shirts to lip balm from promotions, contests and games including Pachinko, the arcade game that looks like a vertical pinball machine.

"I feel the fair really, really brings in a lot of tourists to visit Harrington and really, really helps the local businesses," Maycee said.

"Without the fair, nobody would know about Harrington," Elle added. "The fair is what Harrington is known for."

They said the fair and Harrington both help give each other a good name – and they love volunteering.

Another thing modern fairgoers can do that previous generations couldn't is become part of the news.

Media companies often broadcast live from the Exhibit Hall and invite passersby to become part of their reporting on the fair. Some even get a shot at the news anchor's chair or doing their own live interviews of other fairgoers.

And they can take selfies at the same time.

Its high-tech and high energy also show that keeping up with the times is an ongoing theme for and at the fair.

Other recent improvements in the area include a new stage and sound system at The Hertrich Plaza in front of the grandstands to create a free-standing performance and activity venue capable of seating as many as 750 fair patrons and hundreds more in the "standing-room-only" areas surrounding the bench seats.

HELPING OTHERS

Maybe the giant shopping cart is a clue.

More than 70 tons of food – roughly up to about 100,000 meals' worth – have helped feed the poor of southern Delaware, thanks to fairgoers and a partnership with the Food Lion grocery stores and the Food Bank of Delaware.

And it's a sign of the times that the Delaware State Fair increasingly looks to give back to the community and builds partnerships with sponsors that benefit both fairgoers and the community.

For the last seven years, the grocery chain and the fair have teamed up to hold "Food Lion Hunger Relief Day," giving free gate admission to any adult or child who donates five items of store-brand non-perishable food.

"When it comes to summer, there's always something to look forward to," the grocery store chain said in a news release. "Whether it's going on vacation, spending the day at the pool or cooking out, the Delaware State Fair is something that Food Lion looks forward to every year."

For the food bank, Food Lion Hunger Relief Day is record-setting help.

Food Lion Hunger Relief Day at the Fair is the state's largest single day food collection drive.

But it has gotten national attention.

In 2017, U.S. Department of Agriculture Secretary Sonny Perdue dropped off donations in person at the state fair to help support the effort and publicize the need to help those who, without help, might go hungry. Other big attention-getters for the food drive are its 8-foot green bean can and that giant shopping cart, which measures 22 feet long, 12 feet tall and 8 feet wide.

The response from fairgoers has been tremendous, said Kim Turner, communications director for the Food Bank of Delaware.

Volunteers at the statewide hunger-relief agency sort donations from the fair and help distribute them through the food bank's network of member programs.

"All of this food will stay in Kent and Sussex counties in Delaware," she said, while joining a bevy of food bank staff and volunteers thanking donors, accepting their canned foods for transportation to the nonprofit's Milford Branch.

Under sun-drenched tents, folding tables held piles of cans – tuna, vegetables, soup, fruit – destined to help fight rural poverty in a state where experts say one in every eight people struggles with hunger and that number goes up to one in every six among children.

In addition to the satisfaction of helping others in need – and getting into the fair free – Food Lion has been rewarding donors with some great freebies created specifically

Above: U.S. Department of Agriculture Secretary Sonny Perdue with Food Lion crew for Hunger Relief Day donors – cutting boards, sunglasses, cell phone stands, veggie peelers, light sticks and coupons for $5 off groceries.

"We love doing this, coming out to the fair to help people and show Food Lion cares," said company representative Bob Mills, adding the partnership is a significant priority for the grocery group.

"The Food Bank of Delaware is proud to partner with the Delaware State Fair in Food Lion Hunger Relief Day," said Patricia Beebe, the food bank president and chief executive officer.

"Since the first year of our partnership in 2012, we have raised over 145,000 pounds of food to date collected from Fair attendees," Beebe said after the last fair.

The partnership has added a new dimension to the fair for Chad Robinson of Harrington.

"I can't remember a year in my life I haven't been here at the fair every day," he said. But now, he is communications manager for the Food Bank's Milford Branch, so his fair experience is that much richer.

In addition to distributing that food to the needy who live in

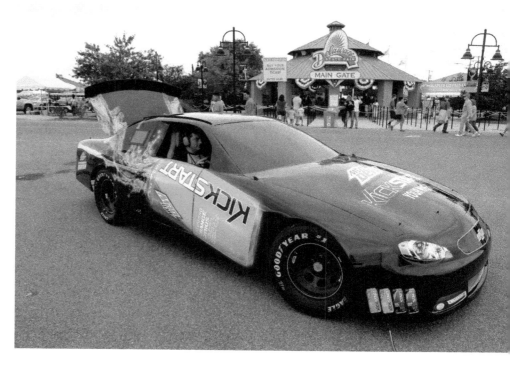

Kent and Sussex counties, the hunger-relief program's partnership with the fair has expanded.

"Our chefs and nutrition educators conduct cooking demos at the Fair, and the FFA and 4-H both donate fresh Delaware-grown produce to the Food Bank," Beebe said.

"The Delaware State Fair is such an integral part of the landscape of Delaware and such a rich part of Delaware history," she added. "We are proud to be a part of a community that is so generous by giving back to their neighbors in need. We wish the Delaware State Fair congratulations on celebrating their first 100 years and we look forward to being a part of writing the history of the next 100 years."

GIMME A BREAK

Each and every person who owns stock in the Delaware State Fair – more than 4,200 shareholders in total – enjoys a fabulous perk that is the ultimate price break on admission to the fair.

Stockholders get in free every day of the fair they want to attend. And, as long as they own at least one share, it's a perk that lasts a lifetime.

Price breaks on admission are a tradition that dates from the very beginning of the fair, with Hunger Relief Day being the latest. They began with Children's Day, intended to give large farm families a break getting in together.

More or less, the fair has kept its admission fee about the price of going to a movie. When the fair began in 1920, online comparisons say a movie ticket cost about a quarter – exactly the same as adult fair admission. Nearly a century later, the national movie-ticket average is $10 to $20 for adults and $5 to $10 for children, while general fair admission is $9 for adults, $4 for ages 6 through 12 and free for those under 5.

"The biggest complaint we get by far is the price of tickets, but I tell them about all the discounts," said Harvey Kenton, a longtime fair director and Delaware state representative who announced his retirement as a lawmaker – but not from the fair – in 2018.

Kenton is quick to tick off the various discounts.

There's Pepsi Day for $2 off with specially marked cans; free Food Lion Hunger Relief Day with canned goods; two free Senior Days for anyone 60 or older; free Kids' Day for ages 12 or younger and free Armed Forces Day for those with military ID.

The fair also gives away general admission tickets and tickets for many special events every year as part of promoting the event.

From the start, the fair's organizers were committed to keeping the event affordable, knowing that farm families like their own often had little or no money for much of the year.

In modern times of families stretching every dollar, one news report said a hypothetical family of four with two adults could spend a day at the fair for as little as $26 and enjoy exhibits, livestock and such free

activities as yoga with goats, a camel show and circus, along with a petting zoo and free musical performances.

Families also could scale up what they spent based on their budgets, the 2018 report said, to a total of about $460 for the day with unlimited midway rides, helicopter rides, state fair shirts and other souvenirs, a headliner show and as much fair food as they all could eat.

Still, those calculations didn't factor in any special free-admission days, ticket discounts or free admission if the hypothetical children were 4 or younger.

Single-ride ticket sales are available, but families are the main customers for a wide variety of ride discounts. Details of those wristband offers vary, depending on the day of the week, how unlimited ride bands are bought and available coupons.

The fair also maintains free parking, a special drop-off area for those with disabilities and free shuttle service. For fairgoers' convenience, there also are rentals of various mobility devices and automatic teller machines that are certified safe and monitored near the fair entrance.

But "The Blue Ribbon Guide to Savings" offers the ultimate opportunity for savings-minded fairgoers.

Modeled after discount coupon books for restaurants and entertainment, "The Blue Ribbon Guide" began in 2017 by offering $400+ in savings. With its price kept steady at $10, the guide racked up $2,400 in coupon and discount offers just one year later.

After getting free admission by donating canned goods on Food Lion Hunger Relief Day, the Blue Ribbon Guide coupon book was the first thing one fairgoer wanted.

Once she wheeled her baby carriage through the gate, she stopped immediately at the information pavilion – fair map in hand – to ask where to buy one.

When she was told to go to the fair's Administration Building, she turned her baby carriage quickly, but stopped abruptly with another question:

"Are they still only $10?"

When she got a "yes" answer, she rocketed away with a loud "Woo-HOO!"

PUBLIC SERVICE

A growing number of fair sponsors are focusing on providing help from a free watering station for service dogs and other service animals, to the First Aid Station with a breastfeeding station. And a Rain Room lets fairgoers cool off in hot weather.

At the Judges Chambers, a volunteer's initiative collects soda can pop tabs for the Ronald McDonald House of Delaware, which provides free lodging and meals to out-of-state families that are visiting while their critically ill children receive medical treatment here.

Another big help on the fairgrounds gets a lot of thumbs up – and bottoms up.

That's a free baby-changing station that provides wipes, diapers, friendly support and to-go samples, all courtesy of the Procter & Gamble baby wipes plant in Dover and its employees.

On Children's Day at the fair, they can go through hundreds of diapers, along with all the related products, said station volunteers Jason Gibbs and Jim Moore.

"We've had tiny little babies up to older kids," Gibbs said.

"People really appreciate what we do," Moore said, both at the fair and at the plant.

When one mother pushed up a stroller with her little baby, she already knew how the free diaper station worked.

That's because, just the year before, she was there with the same baby.

"It was her first time at the fair," the mother said. "She was only four days old."

She said it was great to see the volunteers swing into action when she put her baby on the changing table.

One of the men checked the baby's size, grabbed the right diaper from a stack and handed it with a pack of wipes to the other volunteer, who finished the clean-up and change with precision and gentleness.

"I think this is just awesome," the mother said.

LOST & FOUND

Time was, one of a fella's tools might fly out of his truck as it bounced along the fair's dusty, rutted roads in their days before paving. Or a gal's fancy hanky might take to the wind as she spun on the Tilt-a-Whirl.

Above: Delaware State Fairgrounds 1977, corner of U.S. 13 and Fairground Road

Nowadays, there's a different look at the Delaware State Fair's lost and found – all things modern.

Is that your smartphone? Your Coach clutch? Dolce & Gabbana shades?

How about your remote-lock SUV key? Your fancy earbuds? ATM card?

"We do everything we can to get things back to people," said Administrative Assistant Caitlyn Cain, who handles the lost-and-found along with her various other duties.

She got most of the found items turned in at the latest fair – stored in a bin kept secure in the Administration Building – back to those who lost them. "But I'm still working on it," she said with her characteristic smile and can-do attitude just after the fair closed.

Although there are no formal records, she figures fair officials have been reuniting fairgoers with their possessions ever since they started losing them, so every year's lost-and-found is a reflection of its times.

Another advantage of modern times: Year-round fair staff boosts chances of owners getting back their things, Cain said. So even after the fair, anyone can call the Administration Building to inquire about a lost item and arrange to send a cellphone photo as proof of ownership to get back what was lost.

Unless, of course, it was their cellphone.

THROUGH THE YEARS

1919

Friends talking around a potbelly stove at Harrington's railroad station decide to start a new fair.

1920

Kent and Sussex County Fair incorporates. Founders sell 1,200 shares at $25 each, buy 30 acres, build a racetrack. Charles D. Murphy Sr. is elected the first president of the fair. Fair debuts July 27-30 with horse racing, competition from canning to cattle, midway rides, shows and concessions. Admission: 50 cents, kids half-price – plus "war tax." Fair's profit: Less than $44.

1921

Fair expands to five days, introduces auto races and fireworks, opens Boys and Girls Club Department, a precursor of 4-H Clubs of Delaware. The state erects a new State Exhibition Hall for agriculture and domestic arts. The fair site expands with the first of many more land purchases. After first taking entries only from Kent and Sussex counties, fair declares itself "Open to the World."

1922

Fair grows to 20 shows, four rides, three bands, 50 trained horses and 100 wild animals. The Horse Department expands to add ponies and mules. Events begin moving to the Harrington fairgrounds from the Elsmere fair, a drain that saps the northern fair's attendance and finances.

1923

In first estimate of attendance, fair is said to draw about 35,000, partly credited to "a high-class vaudeville show." Forecast rain holds off until closing night, then slams fairgrounds, knocking out telephone service.

1924

Fair starts lasting tradition of Children's Day with free admission for youngsters. Special events including parade and pageant highlight agricultural progress since formation of the Extension Service. Activities close at the state fair site in Elsmere, leaving only its racetrack and grandstands in use through 1943.

1925

The booming Kent and Sussex County Fair proclaims itself "Delaware's Only Fair." A 40-acre purchase nearly doubles the grounds, a bandstand is added and organizers report attendance is up 125 percent from 1920. A horseshoe-pitching contest begins. Dr. W.T. Chipman of Harrington becomes a fair director, serving as its doctor until his death in 1960.

1926

Fair stockholders gather for their first banquet. Some are discouraged by the fair starting the year with a cash balance of just $1.01, but are buoyed by growing attendance, entries, entertainment, prizes and grounds. Says one report: "Doomsayers were convinced to forge ahead undaunted." The fair expands to "one solid week."

1927

Fair builds new Boys and Girls Building for $5,700, trims run back to five days. Nationally known Joe Basile's Madison Square Garden Band starts decades' long run at fair, playing for various acts. Fair's founding president, Charles D. Murphy Sr., hands the reins to Benjamin I. "Pete" Shaw, who serves through 1947.

1928

Fair, already providing cots, starts "Eating House" to feed police on fair duty – doubled to eight officers. President Charles D. Murphy Sr. dies two days before the fair, dedicated to him with flags at half-staff. Organizers, although mourning, go ahead with debut of "Auto Polo," like a modern demolition derby.

1929

Benjamin I. "Pete" Shaw becomes the fair's second president and leads a 10-acre expansion that adds machinery exhibit area. Fairgoers get free chances on a Tudor Ford Sedan. Friday attendance skyrockets, as the winner had to be there to get the car. 4-H Club members sell fair tickets in contest awarding calves to the top eight sellers, as the special admissions get nicknamed "calf tickets."

1930

Despite the Great Depression, the fair moves forward, adds another 10 acres with 1929's $3,000 profit. Premiums are increased to a record $8,500 total and a high-wire vaudeville act thrills crowds. The fair holds its first photo contest.

1931

The fair grows modestly as the Great Depression impacts Delaware. New shows, including a Wild West show and New York revue of "dainty delectable dancers" entice fairgoers, as does another car giveaway.

1932

Fair organizers welcome Future Farmers of America, now called FFA. Past fair proceeds fund new buildings, land purchase brings fairgrounds to nearly 60 acres.

1933

Big crowds turn out to see Victor Zacchini in his first time at the far as The Great Zacchini, Human Cannonball. As costs are cut 20%, repairs use old lumber. Evening shows start admission fees and prizes are reduced.

1934

Fair opens "Calf Ticket" sale contest to 4-Hers statewide, with prizes of two trips to National 4-H Convention in Chicago and three calves. In first fairgrounds lease, Ford Motor Company pays $1,500 to use the site for one day.

1935

As finances improve, 638 new seats replace grandstands benches, a new police barracks is built, other buildings get a coat of paint and 100 shade trees are planted. Gertrude Avery's Diamond Review starts 34-year run at the fair.

1936

Fair attendance hits 100,000. First show by Lucky Teter's Hell Drivers is wildly popular despite rain delay. Mule races also debut. Board stops giving calves as prizes in 4-Hers' contest selling fair tickets, gives all sellers 10 percent commission.

1937

The big draw is a "Miss Delaware 1937" contest. Beatrice Harriet of Harrington wins, with the fair sponsoring her in the next Miss America contest. Another highlight: Goats performing, including high-wire tricks.

1938

The fair places its first radio ads on WDEL and WSAL for $100. Lucky Teter's Hell Drivers return. The Revelations of 1938 revue reportedly "delights with costumic and pictorial splendor, sparkles with pretty scenery and enraptures with alluringly lovely girls." A 10-acre purchase adds to fairgrounds.

1939

Governor McMullen, impressed by last year's Beef Cattle Show, personally puts up $200 prize money for the 1939 show. Entertainment includes the Five Herzogs on flying trapeze. Three more acres are bought for the fairgrounds. Stockholders' annual banquet serves full turkey dinners, 75 cents a plate.

1940

Cattle registration is so plentiful, fair officials limit exhibitors to Delaware owners. Lucky Teter's Hell Drivers give a special show the night before the fair opens. The Roxyettes, from New York City's Roxy Theater, wow the crowd.

1941

Cost concerns delay new youth exhibit building plans. Persistent illegal gambling prompts fair officials to hire a new company to provide the midway. Grandstands at former Delaware State Fair in Elsmere is razed.

1942

With World War II, fair directors feel cancellation "would be unpatriotic." They plan a victory theme, agree to dim lights and omit fireworks, but cancel a week before opening after the federal government requests all fairs postpone. Lucky Teter, signed to return for the fair, is killed July 5, 1942, in a crash at the Indiana State Fair.

1943

Fair continues its only closure in its history, must borrow $15,000 to cover ongoing costs.

1944

The war goes on, but the fair re-opens. Admission is free with every War Bond bought there. The U.S. Army asks to lease the fairgrounds in August and September to house 500 German prisoners assigned to work at area canneries. Fair officials comply. The Army pays $2,500 rent plus $129 for insurance.

1945

Two automobile thrill shows headline the fair, one led by Joie Chitwood, whose show would endure at the fair for three generations of his family. Fairground rental continues to house prisoners of war. Their labor is used to install a cyclone fence, shingle the grandstands, improve the art building and do other painting and repair work.

1946

The fair sets Tuesday as Children's Day and Thursday as Governor's Day – both enduring designations. An architect is hired to design an all-steel grandstands. The fair leases its site for 60-day harness racing meet. A tough financial year sees the fair borrow up to $25,000 for bills, repairs and other costs.

1947

Joe Basile's Madison Square Garden Band marks its 20th year at the fair. Hattie Thomas joins the fair as assistant secretary and treasurer, a post she holds for 40 years. Fair finances improve. Harness racing enthusiasts formally establish an association to hold pari-mutuel racing at the fairgrounds, where the group builds the racetrack.

1948

Fair proceeds fund more expansion of grounds, three new cattle barns and addition of training track. Jacob O. Williams starts a decade as fair's third president. The board OKs Sunday auto racing at the fair but cancels after several ministers complain. A first: Chairs are put on the track in front of the stage, numbered tickets are sold for each of the 200 prime spots. Firemen's Day proves popular.

1949

The fair hires T. Brinton Holloway as its first general manager. Two new swine buildings are built and plans begin for a new 50,000- to 100,000-gallon water tower tank. Fair leaders limit on-site beverage prices to 10 cents.

1950

For the first time, high school bands perform nightly concerts, a tradition that continues. The fair board approves spending $30,000 for the new water tank. A special box of seats is added in front of grandstands for disabled veterans to use free of charge.

1951

Fair runs five days, six nights. Fair board votes to discontinue harness racing in favor of rodeo. First Stockholders' Meeting and Banquet is held with fried chicken on the menu.

1952

Daily afternoon rodeos replace harness racing at this year's fair. New metal

bleachers are installed to replace wooden ones, given to the Moose Lodge. Little Richard Enterprises starts fair's longest food vendor run, continuing through fair's centennial. Fair board decides not to let political interests rent concession space.

1953

Delmarva Chicken Festival is held on the grounds a month before the fair. To cover rising costs, admission rises from 65 to 75 cents and grandstands tickets from 85 cents to $1. To save money, fair borrows chairs from local groups. Harness racing returns. Fair income rises 30 percent rise from admissions, concessions, special events.

1954

Previous fair's proceeds help fund massive growth project including new 4,500-seat grandstands, new art building, other improvements. Total investment tops $350,000.

1955

Governor J. Caleb Boggs leads dedication of new grandstands. New era begins as the fair hosts its first "top name talent." Evening show by The Mariners – stars of TV and radio – boosts attendance, up 10+ percent.

1956

Success with headline acts continues as fair hosts final-night concert by teen heartthrob Pat Boone. Proceeds of 1955 fair fund improvements, new cow wash station, infield flag pole, painting projects.

1957

Kids go wild over special fair guests, The Lone Ranger and his faithful companion Tonto. Entrance area, several roads and the grandstands area are paved. Fair honors harness racing association, presents a TV to J. Howard Lyons of Greenwood, owner of record-setting champion Adios Harry.

1958

Jimmy Dean becomes first country star to headline at the fair. For the kids: Popeye. Massive new steel poultry building opens. Stockholders' meeting pays tribute to women's untiring contributions to the fair.

1959

Headliners include teen idol Frankie Avalon. Road paving continues. Plans are approved to add a mezzanine floor to the grandstands. J. Gordon Smith becomes the fair's fourth president.

1960

Top performers include famous guitarist Les Paul and country music singer Conway Twitty. Construction starts on a new restaurant building, the first with heating and air conditioning.

1961

For the first time, the fair expands to a full week. Nightly shows include country musicians Roy Acuff and Tex Ritter, entertainer Minnie Pearl and pop singer Dion, still known for his hit "Runaround Sue." Best seats: $1.75. The Lone Ranger and Tonto return. George C. Simpson is hired as the fair's general manager.

1962

Voting 402-to-15, stockholders adopt the name "Delaware State Fair." The fair becomes third using the name; first was a fair from the late 1800s that ended in Dover in 1901, second began in Wilmington in 1901, moved in 1917 to Elsmere and closed in 1924. A sudden storm on the fair's opening day tears tents, downs signs, topples Ferris wheel. With speedy repairs, fair goes on, with record 88,000 attendance. Custom sign carver David Hasty of Tennessee starts 30+ year run at fair.

1963

Fair debuts wildly popular stock car races. Performers include pop stars Brenda Lee and the Four Seasons. Les Paul returns. Entertainment includes Joie Chitwood's Thrill show and, on Children's Day, Sandy Luce's All-Girl Thrill Show with fancy horseback riding and chariot races. Fair repeals ban on space for politicians.

1964

TV cartoon hostess Sally Starr draws huge crowd on Children's Day. Fair holds first Senior Citizens Day, opens new trailer park and administration building. Enhanced fire alarm system ties in directly to Harrington Fire Company. Another purchase expands fairgrounds.

1965

For the first time, The Righteous Brothers – top headliners – perform two shows in one night. Special feature provides actual trout fishing. Fair adds four new barns, continues street paving.

1966

The fair opens with its first demolition derby, starting a popular and lasting tradition. Antique farm machinery display debuts. Delaware State Grange builds permanent 40-by-60 foot building for food sales. Fair stock, which pays no dividends, splits 10 to 1.

1967

Fair starts "camping in the grove" for trucks, trailers, campers and tents. New 4-H

Above: Sally Starr

exhibit hall opens. Shows star The Four Seasons, The Rascals, Christy Minstrels with Kenny Rogers and Irish singer Dennis Day.

1968

Sally Starr returns. Hank Williams and Cowsills headline. Top concert seats: $2.50. Smokey Robinson and The Miracles refuse to go on as rain starts, show cancels, "very unhappy audience" given refunds. Still, the week's attendance of 130,000 sets record.

1969

50th anniversary fair features commemorative coins, entertainment by Dolly Parton and The Beach Boys. Also popular: first appearance of an all-female auto thrill show.

1970

Future Farmers of America open exhibit area in 4-H hall addition. Jame E. Strates Shows – last U.S. carnival traveling by train -- starts decades-long midway run. Country star Charley Pride appears for first of many times.

1971

Fair begins Armed Forces Day, hosts state's first American Motorcyclist

Above, at left: Governor Russell W. Peterson

Association-sanctioned, professional motorcycle race. Noted carver Jehu Camper heads new show for Delmarva whittlers.

1972

Fair grows to 10 days with $1 admission, free for kids. Improved counting at the gate records 141,268 attendance.

1973

Parking fee of 50 cents starts. Stars include Kenny Rogers, Roy Clark, Howdy Doody. Fair attendance tops 150,000 for first time.

1974

FFA debuts children's barnyard. Tony Orlando and Dawn break grandstands record with 6,232 at their two shows. Fair President J. Gordon Smith donates building in memory of his late son James G. Smith Jr.

1975

Free parking is restored. Batman and Robin highlight Children's Day. Pretty Cow Contest starts.

1976

The fair – led by its new fifth president Robert F. Rider – fetes 200th U.S. anniversary with Bicentennial Day. Disco show by KC and the Sunshine Band sets concert attendance record at 6,767. Fair completes major sewer upgrade.

1977

Fair tries new ideas: country music talent contest, kids' bike and pony races, motorcycle long jump, apple pie contest. Blood, Sweat & Tears headlines.

1978

Ice Cream Making Contest debuts. Fair features first professional rodeo. Pretty Cow Contest becomes Pretty Animal Contest. Attendance dips to about 140,000.

1979

Fair spends record $90,000 on entertainment – including Charley Pride, Crystal Gayle – sets new attendance record at 163,405.

1980

Rising operating costs raise fair admission to $1.50. Stars include Kool & the Gang, Oak Ridge Boys, Larry Gatlin & the Gatlin Brothers. Fair board approves borrowing $150,000 for new show arena.

1981

New show arena opens, features first goat show. Grandstands tickets run up to $10 to cover growing performer fees. Shows include Loretta Lynn, Air Supply, Carter Family, Mel Tillis. Attendance sets record at 177,600.

1982

Fair, with $2 admission, features first ride day promotion. Glen Campbell, Charley Pride and Glenn Miller Orchestra headline.

1983

Attendance tops 200,000 for the first time. Fair adds youth dog show, all-female wrestling show. Conway Twitty sets grandstands show record at 7,079.

1984

Coca-Cola, Hardee's and Skoal become fair's first corporate sponsors. Youth talent show, horse pull debut. Avian flu prompts precautionary cancellation of poultry show. Anna Belle Brown, Frances Hatfield, Marion MacDonald are elected as fair's first female directors. At University of Delaware, Saralee Webb Towers writes "The History of Agricultural Fairs in Delaware," detailing predecessors and the modern dtate fair.

1985

First monster truck show is a smash hit. Poultry show remains suspended, but is later

restored in consultation with agriculture officials. F. Gary Simpson follows his late uncle as fair's general manager.

1986

Fair sets 217,513 record attendance, despite costs forcing admission increase to $2.50. Problems with both fairground wells leave the fair without water but a collective effort gets water to livestock, restores water service in one day.

1987

Grandstands has first sellout as fair gambles on booking mega-star Willie Nelson, despite concern over need to charge $25 for tickets. Other shows include Charlie Daniels Band, Joan Jett. Fair starts Nanticoke Indian Day, free sponsored entertainment daily. Fair raises admission to $3 instead of restarting parking fees.

1988

In an odd distinction, the fair becomes the last played by performer Gloria Estefan after her crew complains about staging. Fair moves older stage to free entertainment area, rents bigger one. Street paving continues, other improvements include water pipes to the grove. William M. Chambers Jr. becomes the fair's sixth president.

1989

In a big year for entertainment, three grandstands shows top 4,000 attendance: The Judds, New Kids on the Block, Tiffany. Carnival popularity grows. Professional planner Gary Bell helps fair develop strategy for its future.

1990

Fair gets first automated teller machine. Performers include Randy Travis, Barbara Mandrell, Ricky Van Shelton – and Milli Vanilli before their lip-syncing scandal. Proceeds of 1989 fair fund many improvements. New attendance record: 243,527.

1991

Stars include The Temptations, Four Tops, Charley Pride. But the fair gets a double-whammy of weather: A steamy four-day heatwave, then days of downpours. Attendance falls below 200,000 for the first time in years.

1992

Rain washes out livestock parade. Still, shows fuel attendance of nearly 240,000 with Vince Gill, Patty Loveless, Alabama, George Strait, others. Kids love the carnival's giant slide. State transportation officials start rail service to the fair. Marketing director Dennis S. Hazzard becomes fair's new general manager.

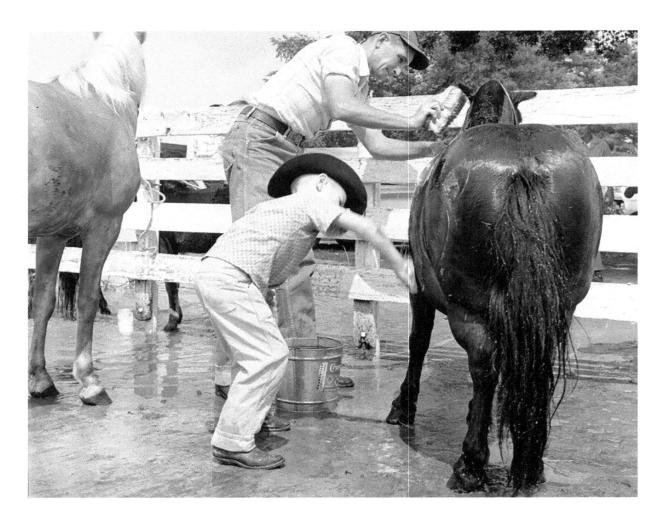

1993

Delaware State Fair is the first inductee honored by state tourism officials' Hall of Fame for annual events, with a plaque presented by Governor Tom Carper. Spam cooking contest is a hit. New attendance record: 243,918, with a record 46,000+ at grandstands shows.

1994

Longtime General Manager Dennis S. Hazzard leads celebration of the 75th anniversary of the fair group's founding in 1919. By now, the fair – recognized as one of the country's best – has 245 acres, paved streets and 50+ buildings. Attendance: 240,000. Delaware Public Archives recognizes Delaware State Fair with state historical marker.

1995

Fair opens with free preview night show by Boyz II Men. Also new: Wild West Days Festival. State lawmakers fund new covered arena. Fair board, main stockholder in Harrington Raceway, votes for track to join Delaware Park and Dover Downs in slots business aimed to boost horse racing. Board President William M. Chambers Jr. casts vote breaking 32-32 tie for measure's approval. Opposition leader G. Wallace "Pat" Caulk Sr., a prominent Republican who was Delaware's first ag secretary, later leaves fair board after nearly 40 years' service.

1996

Slots open at Harrington Raceway, making this the nation's only state fair sharing a venue with a gambling facility. Income from slots helps raceway repay debts owed to the fair, its majority stockholder, and provide funds for ongoing improvements. New fair investments include $400,000+ for restrooms. Economic impact study estimates the fair adds about $4 million to the Harrington area's economy each year. Bill DiMondi becomes the seventh president of the fair.

1997

New Quillen Arena debuts as fair starts a new long-term improvement plan. Fair's new website takes first orders by internet for admission tickets, $5. Attendance for the first time tops 250,000. Midway Slots at Harrington Raceway sponsors World Pro Wrestling, later hosts popular Delaware Lottery area.

1998

New 30,000-square-foot Schabinger Horse Pavilion opens, with housing for up to 180 horses. Shows include Great American Wild West Show. Attendance of 251,841 sets new record. Fair bans laser pointers out of safety concern.

1999

Dusty carnival lot is paved in $1.5 million site improvements. Wade Shows starts as carnival provider, debuts White Water Slide. Fair limits smoking areas. New contests: Lego building, web site design, scarecrow making. Broadway show "Grease" cancels but headliners include Reba McEntire, Lynyrd Skynyrd, Village People. New fair plaza opens, hosts "fair family" wedding. Stephen Hohman, whose family has sold nuts at the fair 30+ years, and Beth Yun, hired in 1998 to help the family, exchange vows and serve fairgoers wedding cake.

2000

New stables open. Construction begins on new poultry building, horse and livestock barns. Fair debuts birthing center, for many years letting fairgoers see livestock being born. Discussion begins about developing a year-round rentable venue for concerts and other activities at the fairgrounds. Attendance count: 254,651. Count of midway attractions tops 50. New book, "Cows, Crops, and Causes: Delaware Farmlife in the 1900s," by Pat and Grace Caulk, highlights the fair.

2001

Fair features All Star Youth Day, antique tractor pull, pig-kiss, Lego and horseshoe contests. Fairgoers try milking a real cow for 25 cents, with the funds going to the FFA, 4-H. Fair sets plan for $4+ million public skating center. Delaware Lottery starts state fair scratch-game, prizes include 23,000+ fair passes. Governor Ruth Ann Minner calls game "the public and private sectors working together in ways that benefit all participants." Rail to the Fair train service by marks 10th year.

2002

The Professional Rodeo Cowboys Association Rodeo packs Quillen Arena. 4-H and

FFA exhibits open in their new home at The Centre, where The Centre Ice Rink later opens as the region's only public ice skating center. Wade Shows brings new rides to fair midway. Fair sets record attendance, topping 275,000.

2003

With constant improvement, "the fairgrounds has changed from a caterpillar to a butterfly," Richard Barczewski, a fair stockholder who chairs Delaware State University's Department of Agriculture and Natural Resources, tells The News Journal. Fair attendance tops 307,000. Record 55,000 grandstands show tickets sold.

2004

Pam and Paul Galyean get married at the fair in a fairy-tale theme wedding, complete with horse-drawn carriage. Special concert series features local talent. New

entrance scanning system counts attendance at record 321,333, up 4.6 percent. Fair officials – partly crediting concerts including sold-out Rascal Flatts show – say past years' counts were too low, missing youngest kids, adults entering free during various specials.

2005

Fair starts concert ticket sales online, also taking online entries. After 2004 sell-out, Rascal Flatts returns for second year, while Toby Keith returns for his third. Other concerts include REO Speedwagon, Lynyrd Skynyrd, Charlie Daniels Band. In lingering heat wave, attendance drops below 300,000.

2006

Pilot project recycles 7,080 pounds of cardboard, 252 of plastic, 135 of aluminum. Peter Frampton headlines, 38 Special subs as warm-up after Foreigner cancels. State police offer free kids' fingerprinting. Special contests: holiday appetizers, gingerbread houses, best-crowing rooster. Demolition derby sells out, concerts by Brad Paisley and others nearly do. Grandstands sets 55,346 record as general admission – $6 for adults – rebounds to 284,436.

2007

Second year recycling doubles plastic, aluminum collection. Autograph-signing Spiderman is huge hit, as is homemade ice cream contest. Other new contests include flip-flop decorating, healthy cookie making. Young environmentalists are honored. Shows include Toby Keith, Carrie Underwood and Daughtry but E-Tickets issue leads to 1,200 invalid tickets, ticketing firm change. Saturday sets all-time one-day attendance record at 40,000+.

2008

Many exhibit categories break entry records, especially vegetables and dairy cows. Carrie Underwood, Daughtry return, other shows include Martina McBride, Lady Antebellum. New firm smoothly handles concert tickets. New state police program trains drivers to avoid truckers' blind spots. LeRoy Betts becomes eighth president of the fair. Bill DiMondi, former president, becomes general manager after Dennis Hazzard retires. Days of 100+ heat melt attendance 10 percent.

2009

90th annual fair features contests in Christmas tree decorating, carving vegetables to look like celebrities, animal dress-up after famous people. Wacky chair contest gives its winner spot on The Ellen DeGeneres Show. Performers include American Idol Kelly Clarkson. Fairgoers donate books for Reading is Fundamental. Heat again plagues fair.

2010

News Journal cites fair as "one of the most notable" events for affordable family fun. U.S. Secretary of Education Arne Duncan joins Delaware U.S. Representative Mike Castle and Senator Tom Carper talking to 4-Hers at fair. Paula Deen show shares recipes, humor. Brad Paisley sets record $59 ticket price. Beach Boys, Lynyrd Skynyrd also perform. Fair offers first ticket discounts via Facebook, Twitter and email blast to 32,000+. Attendance tops 2009.

2011

Fair hosts first home-brew competition. In the midway, Wade Shows signs tell fairgoers their rides are powered by clean and renewable soy-based biodiesel fuel in cooperation with Delaware soybean farmers. Critics blast fair booking of "trash pop queen" Ke$ha, who tones down to give a high-energy, PG-rated show cheered by young fans. Record-breaking heat, repeatedly 100+ degrees, roasts fair. R. Ronald Draper becomes ninth president of the fair.

2012

Fair shares opening weekend with first-time Firefly Music Festival in Dover. Some suggest the fairgrounds and $1 million Harrington Raceway stage someday could host Firefly satellite concerts, camping. Fair's second home brew contest, state's only such sanctioned event, draws 300+ beers. Delaware Air National Guard simulation lets public see what mission flights are like. Fairgrounds starts hosting Ag Week for farmers, scientists, ag professionals.

2013

High heat melts attendance to about 228,000. Fair starts $8 general admission – keeps free parking, petting zoo, circus, etc. – after studying other events' offerings, admission, parking fees. Guests from Delaware's sister state in Japan thank residents for crisis aid, hold free food sampling. Luke Bryan, a 2012 cancel, sells out opening night. Other shows include Rascal Flatts, ventriloquist Jeff Dunham, Canadian rockers Finger Eleven.

Above: Paula Deen

2014

Fair opens new adults-only beer and wine garden, "The Roost," emphasizing Delaware-made beverages and attracts good crowds. New app for Apple, Android smartphones lets fairgoers buy tickets, get special offers, use interactive fair map. Returning stars include Keith Urban. Early announcement of Lady Antebellum show saw ticket sales in time for Christmas 2013 gift-giving. Attendance rises to about 282,000.

2015

Attendance rebounds to about 311,000. Fair starts Craft Beer Festival with Grand Funk Railroad, Delaware trio Lower Case Blues. Butterfly Encounter gets up-close with Monarchs. Due to avian flu elsewhere, fair omits 80+ waterfowl classes. Shows include Bryan Adams, Meghan Trainor. Nanticoke Indian Dance Troupe highlights closing day. Fair bans merchandise that may be offensive, citing Confederate flag for example.

2016

Fair is named U.S.'s third best by SmartAsset.com. Fair creates VIP parking and grandstands options. First pre-opening night concert has Jake Owen. Delaware's George Thorogood & The Destroyers give their first show at the fair. Camping adds 90 spots. Fair installs 16-by-10 video screen by food court, debuts dinosaur exhibit and pogo stunt team. Fair recycling tops 41 tons. Off-season for the fair, The Centre starts a craft brew fest, GOP hosts Donald Trump rally in April at fairgrounds.

2017

TV's Cooking Channel show "Carnival Eats" airs two episodes highlighting fair's food. "Social Spot" opens in Exhibit Hall with social media, selfie-frames, freebies. First fair coupon book offers $430 in discounts for $10. FFA starts youth-led barn tours. Peppa Pig character wows youngest fairgoers. Shows include Rascal Flatts, 1970s' rock revue. "Bumper Cars on Ice" open at fairgrounds' The Centre Ice Rink, fair's Facebook video of the bumper cars goes viral with 750,000+ views.

2018

Fair marks 99th year as "Your Summer Destination," promotes 2019 Centennial. Coupon book, still $10, offers $2,400 in savings and discounts. First Aid Station adds breastfeeding area. Singers Toby Keith and Brett Eldredge, ventriloquist Jeff Dunham return. Circus Hollywood free attraction adds daily camel show. Twiggs the Giraffe stars in free petting zoo. Attendance: 291,316, up 2 percent from 2017 despite heat and rain. New record: Top one-day attendance in fair history Saturday, July 28, at 48,653.

2019

Nonprofit Delaware State Fair marks "100 Years of Family Fun." Exhibition in partnership with Delaware Public Archives honors the anniversary, as fair celebrates with publication of anniversary book, limited edition commemorative coins, many special activities and collectible souvenirs for the July 18-27 fair. With state lawmakers' support, Delaware issues special license plates in honor of fair's 100th year.

THE GREAT DIVIDE

The most difficult chapter of the Delaware State Fair's history was nothing like the crises of lost public interest or financial shortfalls that sank other fairs in the state.

It was a question of gambling – at multiple levels.

As the state moved to allow creation of video-gambling casinos at the state's racetracks – in part to help bolster the fiscally flagging horse racing industry after interest waned over the 1980s and 1990s – Dover Downs and Delaware Park in Stanton welcomed the assist.

At the Harrington Raceway, however, the idea caused a fissure.

The Delaware State Fair then held and still owns about 77 percent of the raceway's common stock, effectively casting the decision about the video-gambling proposal to the 80 members of the fair's Board of Directors.

The issue was one that divided families as well as friendships.

And the decision ultimately would go down as the most dramatic moment in fair history.

Debate also raged at the state level as critics including a variety of religious groups contended the state already had too much gambling.

A slots bill that passed the House and Senate in 1989 was vetoed by then-Governor Mike Castle.

A similar measure reached the desk of the next governor, Tom Carper, who vetoed it.

Negotiations led to a compromise with more state control and, in 1994, Carper declined to sign the bill passed by the House and Senate, then known as the "Horse Racing Redevelopment Act," but let it become law without his signature.

The bigger racetracks, Delaware Park in Stanton and Dover Downs, quickly sought gaming licenses from the Delaware Lottery – legally designated as the gaming regulator – and soon opened their video-based slot machines, while debate continued for more than a year in Harrington.

Acknowledging the fair's difficult decision about whether to adopt the video-lottery gaming expansion opportunities, the state legislation was drafted with a provision for Harrington Raceway to take a pass and instead receive an annual stipend of up to $325,000 funded by the other two tracks and casinos.

The availability of the annual $325,000 consolation prize also fueled opposition to the fair bringing slots to Harrington.

Opponents of the proposal were led by G. Wallace "Pat" Caulk Sr., a prominent area farmer, fair supporter for decades and a longtime board member.

Caulk contended slots would conflict with the fair's basic nature as a family-friendly tradition.

Even though the law mandated that access be limited to adults age 21 or older – like the horse-betting center – critics also were concerned about the influence of the gambling on minors, the potential for gambling to attract bad elements and its possible disruptive impact on the fair itself.

Some said any income generated by the slots would be "dirty money" and should not be accepted.

Others saw the potential benefit to the horse racing community, the racetrack and the fair itself.

The most ardent and impassioned supporter of the fair and raceway seeking licensure as the state's third casino was William M. "Bill" Chambers Jr., who was president of the fair's board of directors when the enabling legislation became law on July 16, 1994.

The debate came at a critical time for the Delaware State Fair. The raceway, which had initially paid the fair rent, couldn't afford it any more. The fair was lending the raceway money to get started every spring and fall race meet, and every time the fair board granted those loans, there were legitimate concerns about whether the raceway would be able to repay them. Some years, the raceway was supported with hundreds of thousands of dollars from the fair.

The fair itself couldn't afford to keep supporting the raceway and needed money itself to sustain its own operations.

"Nearly every building on the 320-acre fairgrounds needed repair," The News Journal later reported. "Some buildings were beyond repair, their wood infested, beams rotted."

"Virtually everywhere you looked, there was a problem," the fair's General Manager Dennis S. Hazzard told the newspaper at that time.

In taking its 1995 vote on the casino question, the board effectively would decide the fair's future.

Strong opinions on both sides divided the directors, while many of them had mixed feelings.

Then their vote came out a tie.

When Board President Chambers cast the tie-breaking vote – in favor – chaos erupted and he quickly ended the meeting.

By casting the tie-breaking vote in favor of the slots, he risked so much including his deep personal friendships with the board's anti-slots contingent.

Soon after the historic vote, it became clear to Chambers that he no longer could serve effectively as fair president. He and a group of pro-slots directors comprised of Charles D. Murphy Jr. and raceway president Jack Walls recruited a similar-thinking director/candidate – Bill DiMondi, a local lawyer and construction material supplier from the Kent County town of Wyoming.

The opposition drafted LeRoy Betts, a local site contractor, as their candidate for president.

The winner of the election to follow would lead the fair through the implementation of slots in Harrington. As that ballot neared, both presidential candidates heavily lobbied the 80-person electorate in the spring of 1996.

When board members cast their written ballots, the fair's sergeant-at-arms, Georgetown lawyer Gene Bayard, reported to an astonished electorate that the vote for president resulted in another tie.

"So much for the concept of moving on," Bayard said wryly when he announced the election's results to the board of directors.

As directors recall, they were riveted in their seats, marveling that such important votes never had ended in that kind of a dramatic tie.

President Chambers called for a second vote, preceded by allowing each candidate a 5-minute speech to rally votes to his side.

When the second vote was tallied, nine directors had changed their votes in favor of DiMondi, who was elected to succeed Chambers as the fair's seventh president.

Shortly after that vote, Caulk quit the board.

DiMondi went on to serve a dozen years as president, before becoming the fair's fifth general manager, following Dennis Hazzard. When DiMondi stepped down as president to become general manager, LeRoy Betts was elected as the fair's eighth president.

"It was a very difficult time," DiMondi recalled recently. "… A great deal of time and energy was spent over the next few years building consensus and trust among the 80-person board of directors that had become so divided on the issue of slots and the casino."

The Harrington casino opened under the name Midway Slots and Simulcast, a name deferential to the annual fair's carnival feature known as the midway.

Harrington resident and lifelong fair fan Clarence Billings – first in line as the raceway's slots opened August 20, 1996 – told a reporter, "I don't think it's hurt the fair any." He reasoned that folks who went for the slots would patronize the fair and vice versa, adding, "If you go, you have to try both."

The fair's payoff was big, despite the looming addition of casinos in Pennsylvania and Maryland.

The early years of slot machines at what's now called Harrington Raceway & Casino generated as much as $2.8 million in annual dividend income for the fair through its raceway stock, plus rent payments for use of the grandstands and racetrack. Local horsemen who owned shares of raceway stock also shared in the unexpected bonanza of quarterly dividends.

According to Raceway Board Chairman Gene Bayard, dividends paid out to all Harrington Raceway shareholders from 1999 through 2014 topped $41 million.

All the money that the fair realized from slots – including stock dividends and rent paid by the raceway – was invested back into the fair, its infrastructure, facilities and programming.

Draper chaired the fair's Budget and Finance Committee through slots' early years and was a champion of the fair creating a strategic financial fund. The fair invested excess income in that fund, which grew over the years to become a true "rainy day fund," meant to keep the fair out of harm's way should unexpected expenses arise.

"We spent and invested all that money very wisely," Draper said.

Over the years, that income did dwindle as nearby states added casinos and the raceway finally stopped paying dividends on its stock, Draper said. The raceway later would grow to have more than 800 employees, add millions to the local economy and house more than 1,700 slots, a simulcast parlor, poker room, table games and sports wagering.

The fair never again needed to subsidize the raceway, which continues to pay the fair about a half-million dollars in annual rent, he said.

Not long before his death in 2002, Caulk – who also served as the state's first Department of Agriculture secretary – said he never regretted his opposition to slot machines at the raceway on the fairgrounds. "I still wish they weren't there."

When Chambers died in 2011, he was remembered as an outstanding business and community leader, honored by Delaware State Police as the owner of the state's oldest towing company.

"Bill Chambers was a person with a vision as to the great potential the fair could realize from the slots," Draper said. "Bill knew first-hand how much the fair struggled financially but, more importantly, how the fair stood to become the finest fair in the mid-Atlantic region with the economic boost to come from the slots."

The fairgrounds' major interior north-south roadway connecting the fair, casino and raceway areas of the grounds appropriately is named in his honor.

"Bill's heartfelt joy was being elected to the Board of Directors of the Delaware State Fair in 1966," his obituary said. "He was elected President of the Fair in 1988 and served in the capacity of President to 1996," the tribute said, noting that he continued on the fair and raceway boards at the time of his death.

"During Bill's Fair Presidency," the obituary continued, "he recognized the dire need to momentarily perpetuate the Fair and Raceway. Through his love and vision for that future and with relentless determination and leadership, Bill assisted the Boards to bring about business changes to develop the Fair and Raceway as it is today."

After his predecessor's controversial tie-breaking vote, DiMondi recalled, fair leaders came together and did their best to heal any lingering division about slots' approval "by being good stewards" of income from the fair's raceway stock, investing the funds in lasting fair improvements from creating new multi-purpose buildings such as The Centre Ice Rink and 4-H/FFA exhibition building that can be used year-round, creation of a new central plaza, a new and permanent stage in the racetrack infield used by big acts performing at fair time, and paving areas of the grounds such as the carnival lot that had been prone for generations to dust storms or mud.

Longtime fairgoers may be used to seeing what fair leaders consider constant improvements to ensure the event's future, but the total impact may be startling to first-time guests on the Harrington grounds.

When leaders of other state fairs visit from around the country, said fair director John Hickey, a Middletown-area dairy farmer, what impresses them most is the quality and extent of the infrastructure.

Having seen other states' fairgrounds and buildings, Hickey said the Delaware State Fair clearly has invested wisely in lasting assets, overall growth and permanent improvements that may tend to leave other fairs' organizers a bit envious.

"We've got buildings superior to all of them," he said. "Our buildings are second to none."

FUN WITH THEMES

When the Delaware State Fair approached three-quarters of a century, organizers proudly proclaimed its 75th anniversary.

After that, the fair added annual themes for its summertime fun.

Themes have been featured in advertising, annual premium books, contests, promotional merchandise and all over the fairgrounds.

For the July 18-27 event in 2019, the theme is "The Delaware State Fair Centennial: 100 Years of Family Fun."

This special anniversary – with a lot of celebration events in the works – also merited a special fair logo.

Take a look at these fair themes and see how many you remember.

1995	75th Anniversary
1996	A Fair to Crow About
1997	Another Year to Crow About
1998	Stampede on Over
1999	Share the Experience
2000	Celebrating the MOO-LLENNIUM!
2001	Hot Fun in the Summertime

2002   Showing our Pride
in America

2003   Rockin' Around the Fair

2004   Once Upon A Time

2005   A Taste of America

2006   Blue Ribbon Days
& Hot Country Nights

2007   Barnyard Beach Party

2008   Lights, Camera,
Blue Ribbon Action

2009   The Tradition Continues

2010   Delaware's Hottest Ticket

2011   Come be a Kid Again

2012   Where Memories Are Made

2013   Celebrate What's Great

2014   An American Classic

2015   Find Your Fun!

2016   A Slice of Summer Fun

2017   A July Tradition

2018   Your Summer Destination

CHILDHOOD MEMORIES

Childhood memories of the fair have been treasured by generations of Delaware, each a singular time capsule of its era.

"I remember when I was 6 years old," said LeRoy Betts of Felton, a longtime fair director and former president. "My father took me over to the fair to see where the prisoners lived."

Nowadays, few may recall those days, when the fairgrounds housed German prisoners during World War II.

The prisoners placed by the federal government were assigned work to help fill the manpower shortage caused by residents' military service.

Above: Chelsea Warren

Betts recalls the prisoners being assigned work at nearby canneries and farms. "When they weren't needed there, they did work on the grounds for the fair," he added.

But what he remembers most was when the prisoners had work assignments at the farm across from his family's.

"We would take them water," he said. Because none of them spoke English, he added, "they couldn't talk to us, but they would smile at us."

It wasn't until many years later that Betts said he came to understand the prisoners' smiles.

"They were smiling because they had their own kids, just like us."

PULLING TOGETHER

In 1986, the Delaware State Fair got off to a fine start.

Then, disaster struck. As the weekend came, back-to-back mechanical problems left the fair high and dry, with no running water.

First, the fairgrounds' large well went dry – a problem that later was attributed to the collapse of a screen.

Then, a smaller well's pump failed.

And on the grounds were thousands of animals that could not go long without water.

Harrington Volunteer Fire Company came to the rescue, repeatedly filling its tanker trucks and running hoses to provide livestock with water. Volunteers also pitched in to make sure every animal had water.

Delmarva Drilling Company was credited for its nonstop crews that got the small well going again with a new pump – and by Wednesday had drilled a new well that was brought online to replace the failed one.

State health officials also were on-site and involved to ensure that the renewed water supply was adequate and the fair was safe to continue operating.

"If ever there was evidence of people working together for the best interests of the fair, this was it," fair officials later said. "Only through splendid cooperation of many people was the fair able to survive and carry out the full schedule of events."

The crisis also was a chance to see "another side of community service work" by firefighters, they said, noting that some of that year's record fair attendance may have been folks coming out to see the temporary water works. "It was quite impressive to see the stretch of fire hose and pumpers from the fairgrounds into town."

The story of that year's water trouble would endure as a lasting example of the fair's sense of community and can-do attitude.

HISTORIC RECOGNITION

ALL AROUND THE First State, special markers recognize and draw attention to important people, places and things with significant roles in Delaware history.

The Delaware Public Archives' State Historical Marker Program is pleased to honor the Delaware State Fair with its own well-deserved marker, said State Archivist Stephen M. Marz.

Originally installed in 1994, the state marker was replaced recently in ample time to be enjoyed by all who attend the Delaware State Fair Centennial in 2019.

The archives also highlighted the new sign in its "Marker Monday"

feature posted on Facebook.

The sign, maintaining the original text of one of the state's earliest markers, briefly summarizes the fair's history:

In 1919 local residents held several meetings to discuss the establishment of a fair. On January 12, 1920, the Kent and Sussex County Fair Association was organized for the purposes of "promoting and encouraging agriculture" and "giving

Above: Bobby Outten, Director; Dave Wilson, Director; Harvey Kenton, Director, and Bill DiMondi, General Manager.

259

pleasures and diversions to the inhabitants of rural communities." The first fair was held in July, 1920. In 1962, this annual event was named the Delaware State Fair to reflect its popularity and statewide appeal. The grounds have also been used for a wide variety of activities and events. German prisoners were housed here during World War II, and regular pari-mutuel harness racing was commenced in 1946.

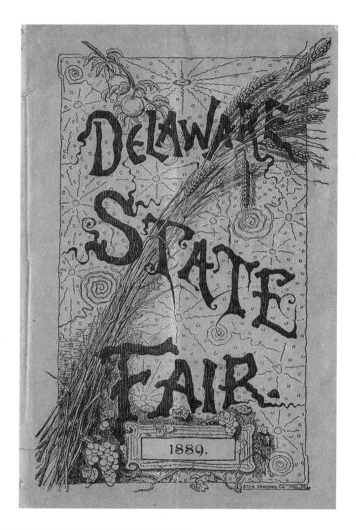

EXHIBIT OF THE CENTURY

A special exhibit at a prominent spot in Dover will celebrate and share the 100th anniversary of the Delaware State Fair.

Thanks to a partnership of the fair and Delaware Public Archives, the interactive exhibit – with memorabilia, old photographs, documents and souvenirs for guests – will highlight the first century of the fairgrounds and encourage visitors to attend the centennial celebration.

The exhibit will reflect the fair's history and heritage, along with the annual anticipation and excitement it brings, say Corey Marshall-Steele, the archives' Marketing / Exhibits Manager & Public Information Officer. "We are thrilled about the exhibit and how much fun it will be," he said.

In the lobby of the Delaware Public Archives, across Martin Luther King Jr. Boulevard North from Legislative Hall, the exhibit — complete with the carousel horse Little Richard gave the fair — will run through the opening of the centennial fair. Details about the exhibit will be posted on the archives' website at Archives.Delaware.gov and on its Facebook page.

The exhibit also will be featured through the archives' popular daily Facebook post, Delaware Snapshot, which has special plans to highlight the 2019 Delaware State Fair.

PAGES FROM THE PAST

These photos, by many different photographers and from a variety of donors, are preserved for future generations to enjoy in collections of the Delaware Public Archives, along with many other historic images throughout this book. Most of these old photos are undated, with no details recorded about the people, animals and activities they show. Still, we hope you enjoy this informal scrapbook of glimpses from the Delaware State Fair's past.

NUMERLS STUDIO
NEWARK, DEL.

Tri-County 4-H Club

THE TEN CORN
COMMANDMENTS

Thou shalt harvest thy seed corn
before freezing weather

II Thou shalt store thy corn properly

III Thou shalt test thy seed

IIII Thou shalt grade thy seed corn
for the planter

V Thou shalt improve thy seed by
selecting the best ears

Thou shalt not import thy seed corn
from a distance

VII Thou shalt treat thy seed corn for
disease

VIII Thou shalt properly feed thy corn

IX Thou shalt rotate thy crops

X Thou shalt practice proper cultivation

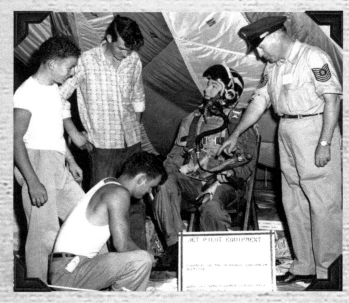

JET PILOT EQUIPMENT

KENNETH WEST
BRIDGEVILLE DEL.

WHAT'S IN A NAME?

OVER THE FAIR's first century, millions of fairgoers have walked along its streets and into its buildings.

But amid the fair's excitement and hubbub, names on many of those roads and facilities may go unnoticed by passersby. Or if seen by visitors, they may go unrecognized.

Each of those names, however, has a significant connection to the fair. Each naming at the fairgrounds – including honors for its early presidents – was intended as a permanent tribute to recognize and memorialize the individual's impact and legacy as well as deep personal commitment and dedication to its success.

However, about 15 years ago, fair leadership decided to stop naming buildings, barns, roads or other features after individuals, to avoid potential hurt feelings or criticism suggesting one person's level of service to the fair was more significant than that of another.

Instead, leaders opted to stick with safe, controversy-free geographical names. So everyone knows those names – Delaware Building, Delmarva Building and the New Castle, Kent and Sussex Barns. But here are explanations of less-familiar names on the grounds.

Above: Harriet E. "Hattie" Thomas

THURMAN ADAMS PADDOCK

Thurman Adams was one of the fair's most ardent supporters in the state Legislature and the longest serving senator in state history. A fair director, he also served as president of Harrington Raceway when that was not a popular position. He led his family's farm and grain business, T.G. Adams & Sons Inc., Bridgeville, and was active in many groups. First elected to the Senate in 1972, the prominent Democrat was president pro tempore and executive committee chairman when he died in 2009.

BOB BENNETT PHOTO GALLERY

Robert J. Bennett was the first official photographer of the Delaware State Fair. A civic activist and firefighter, he also served as postmaster in Rehoboth Beach and Dover. He began photographing the fair and Delaware farm life many years before he became a fair director in 1993. Shortly after he died in 2006 at age 76, the fair board created a gallery of his photos in the Judges Chambers. A separate chapter of this book also shares many of his pictures.

CHAMBERS ROAD

The road from the fairgrounds main gate is named for the late William M. Chambers Jr., who joined the fair board in 1966, served as president in 1988-1996 and cast the tie-breaking vote in favor of allowing slot machines at Harrington Raceway. Their addition generated millions of dollars for the fair, the raceway's majority shareholder, and helped ensure the fair's financial future.

FFA JOHN CURTIS SR. BARNYARD

In 1993, the FFA Children's Barnyard honored its 25th anniversary with dedication to its founder, John M. Curtis Sr. of Harrington. A grain and vegetable farmer who also produced pork, he taught vocational agriculture from 1945 to 1972. He brought animals for the petting zoo and got fellow teachers to help. The beloved barnyard now shares agriculture education in his memory. The World War II veteran, awarded the Bronze Star, died in 1998 at age 79.

HOLLOWAY STREET

In 1949, T. Brinton Holloway of Harrington became the fair's first general manager, handling day-to-day functions, bookkeeping and grounds supervision. A prominent figure in harness racing, he was a leader in many racing and community groups. He also led Harrington Raceway's major expansion in the 1950s. When he died after surgery in 1961 at age 50, fair leaders called him "an untiring and faithful worker... [who] would be greatly missed."

JUDGES CHAMBERS

The VIP lounge is called the Judges Chambers in honor of Paul Neeman, a longtime Kent County magistrate and 1945-1995 fair director. He led the Entertainment Committee and began the fair's firefighters parade. A firefighting leader, Neeman was Harrington Fire Company chief, Delaware Fireman of the Year and a Delaware Firefighters Hall of Fame inductee. He died during the 1995 fair at age 76. The Bob Bennett Photo Gallery is in the Judges Chambers.

MANN-THARP PAVILION

Alfred Mann was city manager and three-term mayor of Harrington, also a public works specialist in Harrington, then Dover. Retiring, he worked for the fair in planning, was a director and played a key role in its 1990s' master plan. He died in 2007 at age 84. The pavilion also honors the family of his late wife Lucille Tharp Mann, including her father, fair founder D. Beniah Tharp, and mother, Nora, who served as a department superintendent for decades.

MESSICK AVENUE

This street in the popular Machinery Lot was named in 1988 to honor Walter Messick's vast contributions to the fair, partly as a vice president in 1969-1988. He was a huge fan of auto racing. His family's John Deere tractor dealership – Taylor & Messick – to this day remains a dominant presence in the fair's agriculture machinery. The company's free Messick Agricultural Museum shows antique John Deere tractors and equipment at 325 Walt Messick Road, Harrington.

MURPHY STREET

Democratic state Senator Charles D. Murphy Sr. of Harrington – eyed as a contender for governor – was the fair's first president, some say its "originator." After a fatal fall, he was buried opening day of the 1928 fair. A record crowd of 8,000 stood in a silent 5-minute tribute. The Wilmington Morning News front page said he had the largest funeral in downstate history and was "known not only for his business qualities but for his many charitable acts."

QUILLEN ARENA

Representative G. Robert "Bobby" Quillen – a Harrington Republican and fair director since 1988 – was the driving force for the $1+ million arena with his name. The state had no indoor horse show site in 1992 when he convinced lawmakers to fund one at the fair. Costs rose, so it debuted in 1995 without bleachers or bathrooms. When Quillen died in 2004 at age 75, he was the only state representative whose service had spanned five different decades.

RAUGHLEY STREET

Ernest Raughley of Harrington was one of the fair's founding fathers. He served as association secretary from its inception, handling day-to-day operations until he died in 1948. He was in the insurance business and active in fraternal and civic groups, including as a Harrington Rotary Club founder. "Much of the success of the fair was due to his untiring efforts and devotion," an official fair tribute said after Raughley succumbed to illness at age 56.

RIDER ROAD

East Street was renamed in 1988 for outgoing president Robert F. Rider, to honor achievements in his dozen-year presidency, including the fair's financial health. Rider was chairman, president and chief executive officer of O.A. Newton & Son of Bridgeville, as well as a director or trustee for other companies and interests such as Wilmington Medical Center. He also served on University of Delaware's Board of Trustees, chairing the building and grounds committee.

SCHABINGER HORSE PAVILION

One of the fair's largest buildings, the state-of-the-art pavilion opened in 1998 is named for Edward H. Schabinger of Middletown, who died in 2007, and his late father, J. Harold Schabinger. Together, their volunteer service as superintendents of the fair's Horse And Pony Department spanned 65 years. One of the fair's longest-serving directors, the elder Schabinger served on the board in 1928-1982 and executive committee in 1955-1982.

SHAW AVENUE

Harrington native and postmaster Benjamin I. Shaw – known as "Pete" – was one of the fair's founding fathers and became its second president in 1929. The prominent

Republican had a produce business for decades in Harrington, where he also was vice president of the People's Bank. He was in his second term as state auditor and serving as fair president and president of the Kent and Sussex Racing Association when he died in 1947.

SIMPSON BARN – SIMPSON ROAD

Houston dairy farmer George C. Simpson joined the fair in 1940, staying devoted until he died in 1985. He was a superintendent, executive committeeman and vice president. He became the second general manager in 1961, praised for his fiscal prudence. A noted Republican, he also was Delaware Farm Bureau president and Harrington Raceway general manager, among other posts. Simpson Road was named after his nephew, F. Gary Simpson, a long-serving director and state legislator who followed his uncle as the fair's third general manager.

SMITH STREET

J. Gordon Smith became a fair stockholder in 1927, director in 1937 and in 1959 was elected as the fair's fourth president. His family owned the 30 acres bought for the original fair site. He was a car dealer, Democratic leader and president of Harrington Raceway among other racing groups. He had the distinction of having been Delaware's ninth draftee for World War I. He donated a building to the fair after his namesake son died in a 1971 plane crash.

THOMAS AVENUE

Harriet E. "Hattie" Thomas of Harrington was the fair's assistant secretary and treasurer for 43 years – also serving as exhibit/vendor manager, problem-solver and goodwill ambassador. "People still come to the fair with the same feeling of excitement they had when they were children," she once told Morning News reporter Nan Clements. "It has a way of getting into your blood. I love it more every year." Retired in 1987, she died in 2000 at age 92.

WILLIAMS STREET

Jacob O. "Jake" Williams became the fair's third president in 1948 after serving as a director, with four years on the executive committee. He was known for his work promoting the fair to achieve the traditional slogan adopted in its second year, "Bigger and Better." Williams led a $10,000 expansion of the grounds with fair proceeds funding addition of three properties. He served as president until his death after a long illness in 1958 at the age of 76.

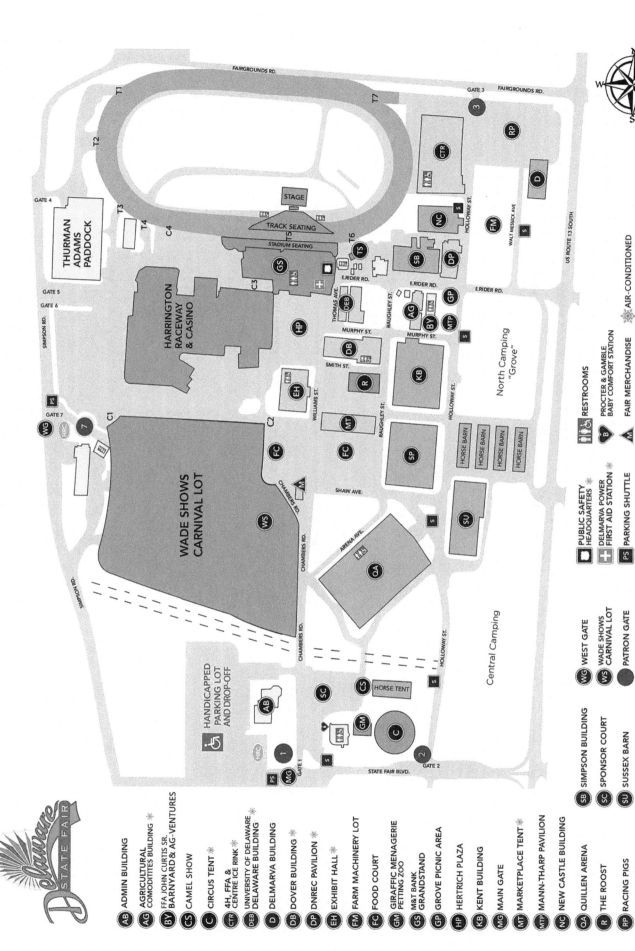

Delaware STATE FAIR

FAIRGROUNDS RD.

THURMAN ADAMS PADDOCK

STAGE
TRACK SEATING
STADIUM SEATING

HARRINGTON RACEWAY & CASINO

WADE SHOWS CARNIVAL LOT

HORSE TENT

North Camping "Grove"

Central Camping

HORSE BARN
HORSE BARN
HORSE BARN
HORSE BARN

HANDICAPPED PARKING LOT AND DROP-OFF

STATE FAIR BLVD.

GATE 3
GATE 4
GATE 5
GATE 6
GATE 7

SIMPSON RD.
FAIRGROUNDS RD.
US ROUTE 13 SOUTH
WALT MESSICK AVE
HOLLOWAY ST.
RAUGHLEY ST.
THOMAS AVE.
WILLIAMS ST.
CHAMBERS RD.
E. RIDER RD.
MURPHY ST.
SMITH ST.
SHAW AVE.
ARENA AVE.

Legend:

- **AB** ADMIN BUILDING
- **AG** AGRICULTURAL COMODITITES BUILDING ❄
- **BY** FFA JOHN CURTIS SR. BARNYARD & AG-VENTURES ❄
- **CS** CAMEL SHOW
- **C** CIRCUS TENT ❄
- **CTR** 4H, FFA & CENTRE ICE RINK ❄
- **DEB** UNIVERSITY OF DELAWARE DELAWARE BUILDING ❄
- **D** DELMARVA BUILDING
- **DB** DOVER BUILDING ❄
- **DP** DNREC PAVILION ❄
- **EH** EXHIBIT HALL ❄
- **FM** FARM MACHINERY LOT
- **FC** FOOD COURT
- **GM** GIRAFFIC MENAGERIE PETTING ZOO
- **GS** M&T BANK GRANDSTAND
- **GP** GROVE PICNIC AREA
- **HP** HERTRICH PLAZA
- **KB** KENT BUILDING
- **MG** MAIN GATE
- **MT** MARKETPLACE TENT ❄
- **MTP** MANN-THARP PAVILION
- **NC** NEW CASTLE BUILDING
- **QA** QUILLEN ARENA
- **R** THE ROOST
- **RP** RACING PIGS
- **SP** SCHABINGER PAVILION

- **SB** SIMPSON BUILDING
- **SC** SPONSOR COURT
- **SU** SUSSEX BARN
- **TS** TRACK / STADIUM ENTRANCE

- **WG** WEST GATE
- **WS** WADE SHOWS CARNIVAL LOT
- ● PATRON GATE
- **HRC** HARRINGTON RACEWAY & CASINO INFORMATION TENT

- 🚻 RESTROOMS
- **B** PROCTER & GAMBLE BABY COMFORT STATION
- 🎡 FAIR MERCHANDISE
- ❄ AIR-CONDITIONED
- ▦ EXHIBITS
- ▦ LIVESTOCK
- 🎭 ENTERTAINMENT

- ▣ PUBLIC SAFETY HEADQUARTERS
- ✚ DELMARVA POWER FIRST AID STATION ❄
- **PS** PARKING SHUTTLE
- **S** SHUTTLE STOP

THE GRAND FINALE

Fireworks have been a fan favorite, consistently popular since they made their debut at the fair.

Fairgoers, like other fans of fireworks, don't care about their murky history.

No one knows exactly where fireworks were invented, with the longtime assumption of China being challenged with arguments for India and the Middle East. But sometime around 800 A.D., invention of the first rudimentary gunpowder marked the start of fireworks as we know them today.

Gunpowder was the unintended consequence of early experimentation, historians say, but once the addition of rockets made bright blasts in the sky hundreds of years later and addition of chemicals created a range of colors, the explosives originally used to ward away evil spirits became great entertainment.

After the tremendous success of the first Kent and Sussex County Fair, organizers had little hesitation about what they would add to draw big crowds to the second one: Fireworks.

Although they mainly are associated with the Fourth of July and considered many events' "grand finale," officials say they are planning for the fireworks display at the Delaware State Fair Centennial to top any in the fair's history.

And, while marking the grand finale of the fair's first 100 years, the fireworks also will launch the Delaware State Fair spectacularly into its second century, ever echoing the slogan adopted in its second year –"Bigger and Better Than Ever."

FUN FIREWORKS FACTS

Everyone who likes fireworks knows what a blast they are – literally – but this condensed list shares Smithsonian Magazine's fun fireworks facts.

- The Chinese used firecrackers to scare off mountain men. Bamboo stalks left too long on coals exploded and, Scientific American says, Chinese scholars noticed as early as 200 BC that the noise would scare away large mountain men.

- The invention of fireworks led to invention of pyrotechnic weaponry, not the other way around. By 900 CE, Chinese alchemists, supposedly trying to find an immortality elixir, mixed the ingredients creating crude gunpowder. The first gunpowder weapons were recorded in 1046.

- Fireworks are just chemical reactions. They simply require ignition of three key components — an oxidizer, fuel and color chemicals.

- Specific elements produce specific colors. Copper produces blue, strontium and lithium make reds, titanium and magnesium burn silver or white, calcium produces orange and barium burns green.

- China may have invented fireworks, but Italy invented the colors and aerial display. Italians developed the launching aerial shells in the 1830s and added metal powders for color.

- Marco Polo probably wasn't first to bring gunpowder to Europe. He brought fireworks from China in 1295, but historians argue Europeans likely knew of them from the earlier Crusades.

- Sound comes from an addition to fireworks' recipes. Aluminum or iron flakes hiss and sizzle, while titanium powder booms.

- Fireworks are poisonous, dangerous, can't be recycled and aren't for everybody. They release pollutants and leftover cardboard typically isn't recyclable. Fireworks cause 10,000+ injuries annually. They also frighten pets and some people.

- Fireworks have been used in pranks for centuries. Pranks even led Rhode Island to outlaw use of fireworks for mischievious ends in 1731.

- Americans have set off fireworks to celebrate independence since at last 1777. That year, historian James R. Heintze wrote, celebration involved 13 cannons, fancy dinner, toasts, music and, a newspaper reported, "a grand exhibition of fireworks, which began and concluded with thirteen rockets."

POETIC PRAISE

MANY HAVE WRITTEN about the Delaware State Fair, from stories published in community newspapers to the tribute cast in the metal of a state historical marker from the Delaware Public Archives.

Twice, the fair earned the praise of poets.

The first was published in the 1957 premium list, before the Kent and Sussex County Fair was renamed as the Delaware State Fair.

"WHO AM I?" was printed without the author's name, which, sadly, has been lost to time.

The second poem initially was published in the 1962 premium list.

It was written by Marguerite Eleanor Weaver of Wilmington, who had the distinction of being appointed that year by Governor Elbert N. Carvel as Delaware's seventh poet laureate. Her other works include "Salute to Gettysburg."

WHO AM I?

I am one of Delaware's most powerful forces.

I am neither the Butcher, the Baker, nor the Candlestick maker

I am the combined efforts of all these men.

I am the barometer of Civic Prosperity.

I exist not for the personal glory of men.

I exist for the good of the Community.

I recognize no Creed, no Religion, no Politics.

I recognize every man alike.

I exist by the efforts of men of Faith and Social Standing.

I belong to the people of Delaware.

I am the spirit of the Community.

I AM THE KENT & SUSSEX FAIR
DELAWARE STATE FAIR

A sparking jewel within the crown

of Delaware, attracts from farm and town

to Harrington, where all is impelled

to present a Fair still unexcelled.

Inside the circle of rich green land

is gathered the harvest we command.

Displays invite you to ramble there

to see the First State's production fare.

Judges are ready with ribbon and bow

on the best of exhibits to bestow.

Competition keen – many partaking

vie for honors in homemaking.

Farmers around show the best of breed –

learn also about the latest seed.

Tractors, plows and every machine

show how to lighten daily routine.

Races are ready to bring to the fore

the finest pacers and trotters galore.

Performers and hawkers are in a gay mood.

Delmarva's famed chicken is succulent food.

Thus – is offered for your pleasure

bountiful things in true measure.

Our Governor adds his full share

of honors bestowed on the Delaware State Fair.

SOURCES

IN ADDITION TO those quoted from 2018 and 2017 interviews, these sources were helpful in research:

City of Harrington website
Delaware Auto Racing, Chad Culver and Wayne Culver
Delaware Department of Agriculture, various materials
Delaware State Fair, diverse materials and media
Delaware State News, multiple dates
Delaware Today, assorted dates
The Delmarva Farmer, American Farm Publications, August 10, 2018
The Dover Post, various dates
Essential Pittsburgh, 90.5 WESA, "Why Doesn't Pennsylvania Have a State Fair?"
Fairs and Expositions, November-December 1988
Hagley Museum and Library
The Harrington Journal, several dates
Harrington Historical Society
Harrington Raceway & Casino, casino.harringtonraceway.com
"History of the Delaware State Fair, formerly Kent and Sussex County Fair," Delaware State Fair, 1994
"The History of Agricultural Fairs in Delaware," Saralee Webb Towers, University of Delaware, 1984
Hoofbeats magazine, July 2001
The News Journal, archived articles, various dates
Kent County Tourister, Winter 2001
LiveScience, The History of Fireworks, Alina Bradford, 2018
The Milford Chronicle, multiple dates
"Mispillion Forest, A History of Harrington, Delaware and Area," Greater Harrington Historical Society
National Association of Agricultural Fair Agencies
The News Journal archives
Readers.com, readers.com/blog/biggest-state-fairs/
Smithsonian.com, 14 Fun Facts About Fireworks, July 4, 2014
Tech Republic, techrepublic.com
Town of Elsmere website
Travel & Leisure, travelandleisure.com/best-state-fairs
U.S. Census
U.S. Geological Survey, Geographic Names Information System

ACKNOWLEDGMENTS & SHOUTOUTS

This book celebrating the Delaware State Fair Centennial would not have been possible without the remarkable support and assistance of the fair's dedicated officers and directors, Centennial Committee and staff members.

Partnership with the Delaware Public Archives has been instrumental to this book's creation as well as the sister exhibition. Special thanks go to State Archivist Stephen M. Marz, Marketing/Exhibits Manager & Public Information Officer Corey Marshall-Steele and exhibit team members Tammy Stock and Carlos A. Maldonado.

Also appreciated is the generous cooperation of the Harrington Historical Society, its mother-son duo of Viva and Doug Poore, countless fairgoers and volunteers. We also thank Sandra Eichbaum for graciously sharing information about her relatives involved in the fair for generations, including Alfred Mann and D. Beniah Tharp, for whom the Mann Tharp Pavilion is named.

We also acknowledge photographers whose pictures are shared in this book, including Ralph Freso, Jason Minto, Austin Wright, Christy Hermongenes and Jon Lloyd.

THANKS TO OUR SPONSORS

The Delaware State Fair gratefully acknowledges and thanks all the generous individuals, businesses and other organizations that have sponsored a wide variety of different attractions, activities and facilities over the years. In many cases, this support has spanned generations. Fair sponsors have, from the start, proven to be a vital – and deeply appreciated – part of the fair's success and fairgoers' entertainment experience, as well as a crucial support in the fair being the only one in state history to reach a century of providing family fun and community enrichment to Delaware and beyond.

FROM THE AUTHOR

I HOPE EVERYONE ENJOYS this book celebrating of one of my favorite Delaware traditions.

Being chosen to create the centennial book is one of the greatest honors and joys of my life.

I thank leaders of the Delaware State Fair and Delaware Public Archives for this opportunity.

And I thank the fair's dedicated directors and others who contributed to this book, as well as to the fair itself. My love of the fair has grown thanks to all of you and this year of research, interviews and writing.

Thousands of folks, many long gone, have made the fair what it is today and will be in the future.

My love of the Delaware State Fair began with childhood days in the Greenleaf 4-H Club.

My first blue ribbon from a poultry project hangs in my kitchen now, near an apron that was my first sewing project using Mom's machine. My brother Chris and I still share old 4-H and fair quips all these decades later.

In my 40 years with The News Journal, I loved writing about the fair and fairgoers. One of my favorite stories let people know an orangutan was coming to pose for pictures with people at that year's fair. On Reginald the Orangutan's debut day, I put on my high school gym suit, pearls and pith helmet, then drove to Harrington. The $5 photo was worth every mile and every penny. Reginald remains the star of my favorite Christmas photo card: "Jungle Bells."

To everyone connected with the fair – directors, officers, vendors, exhibitors, fairgoers – deepest thanks for your part in all the fair fun and memories shared over the fair's first century. My deepest personal thanks go to General Manager Bill DiMondi, Assistant General Manager & Director of Marketing Danny Aguilar and Administrative Assistant Rebekkah Conley.

And, of course, I wish the Delaware State Fair continued success, gentle weather and great big, happy crowds in the century to come.

robin brown
Delaware Public Archives
Writer-in-Residence

INDEX